A *Blissful* NEST

A *Blissful* NEST

DESIGNING A STYLISH AND WELL-LOVED HOME

Rebekah Dempsey

ROCK
POINT
QUARTOKNOWS.COM
NEW YORK, NY

Contents

Introduction

WHEN I WAS A LITTLE GIRL, I would frequent flea markets, thrift stores, and garage sales with my parents on the weekends. It was just what we did together as a family. After they retired, my parents became antique dealers, so it must run in my blood! Little did I realize how much these experiences trained my eye, giving me a sense of how to put things together and teaching me about classic design styles.

On these excursions, I would beg my parents for $40 (or less) so I could get items from the vendors to redo my room. I did this every couple of months—I'm sure my parents thought I was nuts, but they indulged me. I would make over my room in a Southwest theme, or with rainbow hearts, or with a black-and-white chic look with turquoise accents. I even went through a phase where I would cut out all the black-and-white magazine pages with supermodel ads from Guess, BeBe, and Calvin Klein and tape them on my wall to create a border around my room. This is how I got my creative juices flowing as a kid, and I thrived on it.

At age twelve, I declared that I wanted to be an interior designer, but I was told that the job wouldn't allow me to support my family when I was older. So I went to business school instead, got a degree in marketing, and honestly hated it. It was not creative enough for me.

In my mid-twenties, I went back to school, and this time got that design degree I always wanted. I felt like I was reborn. I had a passion for something and loved my job! I was designing at a high-end residential design firm where I had so many great experiences.

But life, as you know, always throws you a curveball. When I was a new mom, our family went through some of our toughest times. My father passed away after a five-year battle with cancer. My husband lost his job in the 2008 market crash, then tore his Achilles tendon and couldn't walk for three months. I was a brand-new mom trying to navigate working full time to support my family and overcome loss. I was mentally broken.

So what do you do when you have nowhere to turn? I went to my happy place of creativity. I started a blog and began cataloging all the amazing design ideas I loved, as well as sharing things I was making at home to celebrate the joys of having a little one. Never did I imagine that blog, A Blissful Nest, would turn into a career. It allowed me to be that stay-at-home mom I always wanted to be *and* have a design career. I still pinch myself that it worked out so well!

After a few years of sharing ideas for entertaining, I realized that I needed to transition the blog to my true area of expertise, which was interior design. That's when I made the switch to focus on teaching readers how to design a beautiful home on a reasonable budget. Because let's face it: most of us are not wealthy with loads of disposable income, but we all want a home that's full of style and personality, perfectly curated to look pulled together and timeless.

Over all the years of refining my design eye, from the time I was a child, through going to school, and then working in the design industry for years, I've learned some tips and tricks that always hold true when decorating a home. My hope is to share these with you so you have the confidence to tackle every room in your home and achieve the look you've always imagined, without breaking the bank.

The Basics of Design

When you are thinking about decorating a space, you need to keep two things in mind: affordable solutions for the functional problems of your home, and the overall look. Form and function go hand and hand, and in design you can't have one without the other. For that reason, there are three basic steps I always follow when designing a room: purpose, plan, and decorate.

PURPOSE

What is the space used for now and what is your ultimate goal for the space?

The answers to these questions will be different for every room in your home. Think about who will be using this room and whether it will need to transition over time. For example, you may want a playroom to become a game room as your kids get older. Planning for this in advance will help you save money in the long run. Use this step to figure out what you feel is necessary to function effectively in the space, both now and in the future.

PLAN

During this stage, you'll plan how to organize and decorate the space.

Begin by making a list of the furniture, storage solutions, and pieces of decor needed to complete the room. Take into consideration the size and scale of each of these elements, so you know how all of them will fit into the space. Measure everything and make a diagram, then use painter's tape to mark the outlines of your furniture and area rugs on the floor to better envision them to scale in the room. During this step, you'll also think about what specific storage solutions you may need, such as a place to corral toys, store dish towels, or organize utensils. Carefully thinking through the elements you need for the room and making a list will help you focus when you are shopping and avoid buying unnecessary things.

DECORATE

In this last step, you'll implement your final design and shop for the pieces you need to decorate your room.

This is the fun part! This is when you can shop for all the items on your list and see your vision come to life. Use your measurements and diagrams to purchase furniture pieces that will fit. Look for clean, simple lines when shopping for furniture so your pieces can transition over time. Consider height and scale when shopping for accessories, to give variation. Plan a color palette ahead of time to keep you on track. Always add one piece of greenery or a floral element to a space to bring in some life.

This basic purpose, plan, and decorate model will give you a foundation for designing your spaces and help keep you on track with your budget. In the rest of the book, you'll find more detailed guides for each room of your home, but they all come back to these essentials. These are the basic steps to creating your blissful nest!

How to Use This Book

Start with a clear head and a clean slate. Grab some coffee or a cup of tea, a piece of paper, and your mood board inspiration. I love to start the design process in a quiet place where I can just sit and focus on the room I am getting ready to design. No other distractions. Make sure you have plenty of time to soak in the process. Enjoy the journey!

YOUR DESIGN STYLE

Flip to the chapter about design trends and styles on page 136 and go over each one. Which ones pop out to you, and which do you identify with? Rip out magazine photos, or make a Pinterest board, and look for any common themes. Write those themes down and use them as inspiration when you are working on a specific room. This will help you keep your design style consistent and make your home decor flow from room to room.

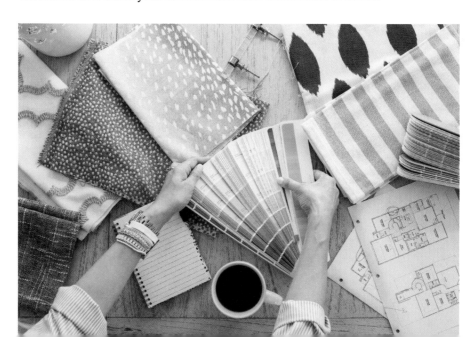

DESIGN PROCESS

Each of the main chapters in this book focuses on a particular room or area in your home. The chapter will take you through the necessary steps to design the room, giving you tips and ideas that are specific to that space. These steps will help you identify your needs as well as aesthetically pull your spaces together. My hope is this will also help you budget and save you money by avoiding unnecessary purchases.

EASY HOW-TOS

I am not known for complicated step-by-step projects. As a matter of fact, I'm just the opposite! In each chapter, I share some of my favorite projects that you can even do with your kids. These are short tutorials on making your space a little more blissful, whether you are in a rental or a new home.

TIPS AND TRICKS

Over the years, I have learned so many lessons the hard way. I have made mistakes that have cost my design business as well as myself. These tips and tricks that I share throughout the chapters are meant to help you avoid those same mistakes and even save some money. They are there to help you troubleshoot design dilemmas and avoid potential problems.

CHECKLISTS

At the end of each chapter, I've included a checklist to walk you through a cleaning or maintenance task for your home—whether it's getting your closet organized or preparing your yard for spring. I hope these will be useful to you even when you're not in the middle of redecorating!

BONUS

In the last few chapters of this book, you will find guides on how to select paint, define your style, and notice trends. At the very end, you'll find a list of where I like to shop online and a spring cleaning checklist. These tools will help you refine your decor and give you my sources for where to find everything. I am spilling my design secrets!

1

Entryway

This is the space that first welcomes in your visitors and greets you when you arrive home after a long day at work. It's so important to make the entryway both functional and beautiful, but it's easy to ignore. With a few simple updates, your entryway can make a great first impression.

W ELCOME HOME! The entryway is the first space someone sees when they walk into your house. I love walking into an entryway, because I can immediately tell who the person is and get a sense of what they like. This might be the most important space to decorate, because it sets the tone for the rest of your home.

Not only does an entryway need to have a fabulous design, but it also needs to function well for the family. Many families use this as a place to hang coats, drop keys, collect mail, hang backpacks, and so much more. The entryway is a key piece of how a family functions on a day-to-day basis.

At the end of the day, it is not just about creating a magazine-worthy entryway: This space should truly represent how your family lives and incorporate your personality.

Purpose

Entryways have different shapes and sizes. Some entryways have huge coat closets and lots of storage space, and some aren't even clearly set apart from the rest of a larger room. Really understanding how a family uses the entryway is the key to designing the space, whatever its features.

In my own home, our entryway does not have a coat closet. I needed to create a place to hang jackets, especially with all the rain where we live in Texas. I turned an unused wall into a place to hang coats right inside the

QUESTIONS TO CONSIDER BEFORE YOU BEGIN

* Do you have a coat closet, or do you need to create a space for jackets on a wall or elsewhere?

* Do you need space for seating?

* Do you need a table lamp, or do you have overhead lighting?

* Do you have space for a cozy rug?

* Do you need a catchall area for keys and mail?

* Do kids need a place for their backpacks or other equipment?

One of my biggest tips is to add texture. You can do this simply by placing a basket next to the entry table for shoes, or by using a burlap shade for your table lamp. This is one of the easiest ways to make your entryway feel warm and cozy.

garage door and really maximized an otherwise wasted space. It wasn't until after we had lived here for a while that I realized how much we needed a space like this. The best design decisions come after living in a home for a bit, so you can get a better sense of how each room in the house can meet the needs of your family.

Before you do anything, you want to determine the purpose of the space and figure out how many areas need to be decorated. Some entryways are long and narrow, some have niches carved out underneath the stairway, and some are just a large foyer space. Does your family have pets, or kids playing sports or in school? Do you need to create storage places for leashes, sports equipment, or backpacks?

There are three main elements I like to address when designing an entryway: storage solutions, lighting, and furniture. When designing your own space, think about where you'll hang coats, place shoes, and drop your keys. Consider where the light will come from, particularly when you first walk into the house. Think about whether you'd like to include a small seating area or any other furniture. You want to create a space that's beautiful and welcoming, but also functions smoothly as you're leaving and entering the house each day.

Plan

Once you know what you need from your entryway, it's time to get inspired and create a plan for designing the space. Since this is the first chapter, I'll walk you through the planning process step by step. Then you can apply these steps to any room in your house.

CREATE A MOOD BOARD

Begin by searching design magazines, Pinterest, and other websites for entryways that inspire you and help you determine what you like. For example, I am not a fan of big, heavy furniture. It can make a space feel dark and confining, especially in a smaller entryway.

Start making your design plan for your entryway with a mood board. Pull colors you like, travel destinations that inspire you, book covers that you love, pictures of patterns and fabrics that move you, and anything else that gets your creative juices flowing. These do not need to be things that will actually go in your space, but rather inspiration for the mood and feel of what you're trying to achieve.

TAKE MEASUREMENTS

Next, take careful measurements of the room. Measure the length of each wall to determine the overall size of the space before you choose any furniture or plan to include other large features.

DETERMINE THE FOCAL POINT

Choose a feature wall—this wall will draw the attention of people arriving in your home. This is where you'll put your most showstopping decorative piece, such as a gorgeous mirror or a beautiful piece of art that you want to showcase.

Choosing a white piece of furniture will instantly make your entryway feel more modern, open, and clean looking. White also goes with just about every design style.

CREATE A FLOOR PLAN

Next, create a floor plan. Using the measurements you took earlier, draw an outline of the design space. Once you have the exterior walls drawn in, start placing the furniture you would like to include in the space. This will help you figure out where your existing furniture will fit and determine the ideal size for any new pieces of furniture you're planning to buy. Also draw in any area rugs you'd like to include—these can be a great way to delineate the different spaces in the room. For instance, in an entryway you may want to use area rugs to define more than one space: one rug right at the door, and then another at the base of a stairwell. Having the space drawn out will help you place the items you already have and determine what you'll need to shop for.

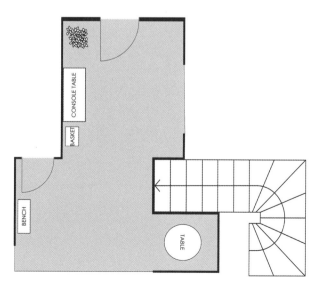

SELECT COLORS AND FABRICS

This is the fun part! Once you've planned the placement of your rugs and furniture, select what colors you want to use in the space. This includes one or more paint colors, but also any fabrics that you would like to feature in window treatments, pillows, and furniture. I typically pick all fabrics first and then identify a color I love in one of the fabrics to use for paint. Pulling a color directly from the fabrics you use in your space will give depth to your design.

SELECT FURNITURE

Once you have figured out which colors and fabrics you're using, it's time to select the furniture pieces you need. Using your floor plan as a guide, look for tables, upholstered pieces, or storage solutions that fit your predetermined sizing. Request finish and fabric samples for any furniture pieces you're ordering to make sure they fit into your design plan. Many companies will mail these to you for free or for a small fee.

SHOP FOR ACCESSORIES

Finally, it's time to accessorize with fun decor pieces that pull in more of your chosen colors and convey your personality. This is when you want to start looking for vases, candles, design books, accent rugs, and pillows to really make your space feel warm and inviting. One of my favorite accessories for an entryway is a beautiful candle, which I light before guests arrive. This not only enhances the room's ambience but also creates a delicious scent that will be the first thing guests smell as they walk in.

BLISSFUL TIP

Shop thrift stores and garage sales for vintage mirrors to brighten the space and add visual impact.

Instantly elevate and lighten your decor in the entryway with a modern white vase or planter with some fresh flowers, like hydrangeas.

Decorate

When you are decorating your space, it's important to identify and stay true to your design style. Keep your personal style as a guiding star no matter what space you are designing. This will give your home a nice flow and the rooms will not clash, which tends to be a problem in the open-concept floor plans that are currently popular.

GIVE IT STYLE

Add personality to your space with art and other small decor pieces. I love to incorporate accessories that reflect my design style. For instance, if you love coastal decor, don't be afraid to show off a gorgeous piece of coral stacked on some travel books about seaside destinations. Try to stay away from trendy decor pieces, like an anchor, and go for more organic and timeless pieces that represent the ocean. If you love boho style, incorporate plants and other natural elements. When selecting decor that echoes a certain design style, focus on the essentials, like color and finish.

PAY ATTENTION TO DETAIL

Because we have such a long and narrow entryway, I was able to create three different areas within it. When you first walk in the door, there is a beautiful Lucite table with a table lamp and mirror. This is where we drop our keys and collect mail each day, and our table lamp lights up at night as soon as the sun goes down—I use a plug-in timer so the light goes on and off automatically. I can't tell you how great it is to have our entryway lit up when we come home at night. Little details like this truly make your home warm and cozy!

Because our entryway is narrow, I selected furniture that felt light and airy to make the space feel more open, and also to reflect my more modern tastes. I also have a little niche carved out at the bottom of our stairs that hosts an ever-changing rotation of decor pieces. I love to switch out the art and small accessory pieces each season. It is such an affordable way to make a space feel fresh and new.

Another detail I love is that our entryway leads into our kitchen and you can see a peek of the art leading into the living room at the far end. Viewpoints like this are why it's so important to make sure your design aesthetic is carried through each space and you have coordinating color palettes.

BLISSFUL TIP

In the entry, use trimmings from your yard and arrange them in a vase as an inexpensive way to bring in the outdoors.

MY FAVORITE ENTRYWAY DECOR BASICS

* **A DELICIOUS-SMELLING CANDLE.** Candles are my favorite decor piece in any room. I love their glow and the scent that creates a mood in the entryway when people walk in the door. They can also reflect the season, with a warm cinnamon apple candle for the fall or a citrus smell for the spring and summer.

* **A FLORAL ARRANGEMENT.** Flowers brighten any space, and I love having a beautiful floral bouquet in the entryway. You can mix fresh flowers and faux flowers for a stunning arrangement. They are also a great way to pop your signature color into the room.

* **A BEAUTIFUL ACCENT RUG.** This is an easy way to add pattern to your space. I look for indoor/outdoor rugs here for durability. They are easy to clean and can withstand the high traffic this space gets.

* **A TABLE LAMP.** I absolutely love having a table lamp in my entryway. It makes my home feel warm and cozy and gives the space some atmosphere.

* **A MIRROR OR PIECE OF ART.** You can't go wrong with a gorgeous mirror or beautiful piece of art in your entryway. A mirror can be a great place to check your lipstick before you head out the door, and a piece of art can add a touch of whimsy.

How to Paint a Door

Repainting your door can be a great way to give your entryway some polish, and the right color will tie your space together beautifully.

Before

After

MATERIALS

* Drop cloth
* Painter's tape
* Sandpaper
* Hand sander with 120-grit sanding disks
* Microfiber cloths
* Primer paint
* Paintbrush, roller brush, angled paintbrush
* Paint

STEP 1 **Prep the door.**

Lay down a drop cloth under the area where you'll be working. Tape off the following areas with painter's tape to protect them from the paint: doorframe, handle, bolt and keyhole, hinges, and peephole.

STEP 2 **Sand the surface.**

Sand the door by hand in the interior of the panels where the sander cannot reach. Once the panels are done, use the sander and sanding disks to sand the rest of the door surface. Move the sander in circular motions up and down the door. Once you're finished, use a microfiber cloth to wipe down the surface and get all the fine debris and dust off.

STEP 3 **Prime the surface.**

With a dark door finish, you will need at least two coats of primer. Apply with a paintbrush or roller brush in thin, even coats.

STEP 4 **Apply paint.**

Start by painting the recessed pieces of your door, then the raised panels. Use an angled paintbrush to get into the crevices. Keep an eye out for drip marks and smooth them out as soon as possible. You can use a larger paintbrush or a roller brush for the rest of the door. A roller brush will not leave visible brushstrokes and will give a smoother finish. Apply two coats of paint and let the paint dry for two hours in between each coat. Depending on how well you primed the surface, you may need to apply a third coat.

Create an Organized Entry or Mudroom

ITEMS YOU WILL NEED:

* Bench
* Baskets
* Hooks
* Shoe organizer
* Runner
* Mirror

Steps to organize your entryway or mudroom:

1. Clear your space and make piles of what you will keep, donate, or throw away.

2. Clean the area by sweeping the floor, wiping down the floorboards, etc.

3. Decide where to place all your furniture, cabinets, and storage pieces.

4. Designate a place for your shoes. These always seem to pile up where you enter the house, so have baskets, a shoe organizer, or cabinet available near the entry.

5. If you have room for hooks, plan for each person in your home to have one or two dedicated hooks. These can be in a closet in the entryway, or you can create a feature wall with wood trim for them to hang on.

6. Use bins and baskets to organize smaller objects like hats and umbrellas. Place these on shelving or in a cabinet or closet.

7. Place a runner inside the doorway—this can help minimize the dirt that comes in from outside.

8. Have a dedicated spot for your keys so they don't get lost, like a hook or basket.

9. Place a bench near the shoe storage to make it easy to put shoes on and take them off as you leave and enter your home.

2

Living Room

A place to gather with family and friends, where you should feel relaxed and at ease, your living room is one of the most important spaces in your home. Find a perfect balance between comfort and style with the design tips in this chapter.

WHEN I WAS YOUNGER, our home was up in the hills in a woodsy part of Northern California. Our living room was on the second floor, and had a wall of windows that overlooked the most gorgeous forest in the backyard. It almost made you feel like you were in a tree house. We spent most of our family time in this living room, and honestly, it's the room I remember most clearly. We would watch movies and play games. I can still remember the day my dad came home with a VCR. It opened up a whole new world of TV watching! We moved out of that magical home when I was nine or ten, and other than my current home, it was my favorite place I've ever lived.

Another living room I will never forget is my grandmother's. It was grand, to say the least! She had very refined taste in decor and I was always scared to touch anything. Glass figurines, polished mahogany, delicate silk-covered chairs—the works. But holidays there were dreamy, and our family was so large that the Christmas presents would cover the expanse of the room, making it the most exciting day. My brother would dress up as Santa and we sat in that living room, drinking and eating the day away with all the gifts. Even though it was a "fancy" room, I still have so many amazing memories with my family there.

If you're anything like me, your living room is a place where you make lasting memories with family and friends. It's one of the most important spaces in your home, and it's worth taking the time to make it truly functional and beautiful.

QUESTIONS TO CONSIDER BEFORE YOU BEGIN

* Do you frequently host guests?

* Does this room need to include a workspace, play area, or other special features?

* Do you have animals that like to jump up onto your furniture?

* Do you have small children and need to avoid sharp-edged furniture?

* Do you need storage solutions for this room?

* Does this space get a lot of natural light or do you need to add extra lighting?

Purpose

The living room, along with the kitchen, is a place most families congregate, where you'll spend a lot of your time. That is why, in my opinion, it's the most important room to decorate first and set the tone for the rest of the home.

When deciding on the purpose of my spaces, I make a list of possible items I should look for so when I'm in the planning stage I can decide what I need. Think about whether you need some desk space in here, or whether you tend to have guests over a lot and may need some extra seating.

Is this going to be a more formal space or a relaxed, laid-back room? Do you have little kids who need toys stored here, or do you want to create a lounge area more suitable for adults? Really thinking about your family's needs and how they'll change over time will help you determine how to use this space.

Plan

Once you've thought through the ways you're going to use your living room, begin planning the details of the space and selecting furniture and other features.

CREATE A FOCAL POINT

Choosing a focal point is an important first step for decorating a room. Decide where you want your eye to be drawn when you enter the room. Is it above the fireplace, or over to one side of the room? How do you enter the room? Will the focal point be straight ahead of you? When you answer these key questions, it helps you define the flow of the room and plan the furniture layout.

SELECT ANCHOR PIECES

Once you have a sense of the room's purpose, flow, and focal point, move on to selecting the main pieces of furniture for your space, or your anchor pieces. Anchor pieces are the largest furniture pieces that will be going into the space, like a sofa, chairs, console table, etc. This is where scale and proportion really are key. To figure out where to place those anchor pieces, draw out solid measurements of the space. You don't need to be an artist to do this—you just want to sketch out the basic sizes of your anchor pieces and their placement in the room. You can honestly just draw them as boxes to get the basic scale down. This will help you select the number of chairs, figure out a realistic size for your sofa, end tables, and coffee table, and place any extra features in the room, such as a workspace or play area.

DEFINE YOUR SPACE

One of my favorite tricks is to use area rugs to define a space. Even if you have wall-to-wall carpet, an area rug on top will make all the difference in delineating a conversation area. I don't like to have furniture pushed up against a wall (except in a bedroom). An area rug can create a focal space where your furniture sits, and mark off smaller areas with a defined purpose within a larger room. I even like to layer my rugs to lend some warmth to the space. As you're planning your room, draw in area rugs where you'd like to define some spaces for conversation, work, play, or any other purpose.

Decorate

A living room is one of the most public spaces in a home, and is therefore a wonderful place to really throw yourself into decorating, highlighting your personal style, and creating a warm, welcoming, and restful room.

Prop a floor mirror on a wall to make a space feel larger and bounce light from a window.

CHOOSE ACCESSORIES

Adding accessories is one of my favorite things to do to a fresh space. The first thing to do is make a list of the items you need, which helps with your budget, so that items you don't need stay out of your shopping cart. Tackle your focal area first. If this is a mantel over the fireplace or a bookcase, do you need a mirror or piece of art? What other accessories, like plants, vases, or candlesticks, might help complete this space?

I love to have extra baskets, cozy throw blankets, plush throw pillows, and decor books in my living room. All these pieces make a room feel warm and welcoming.

I always have something green in my room, like a tall fiddle fig plant in a basket. I generally have this tucked in a corner of the room where it gives a sense of the outdoors coming in. This creates a feeling of calmness, just like being outside can do. If you don't have room for a tall plant, then adding little potted plants around your room will work, too. Tuck these into your bookcase, place them on your coffee table, or add them to your side table.

Another decorating trick for living rooms is to add a vintage piece. It grounds the decor and gives it a sense of history. I love adding pieces that were my grandmother's and mom's. They bring up some of my fondest memories, and I love the mix of old and new. Picking pieces from your local antique store can work just as well, and I often look for things that remind me of the past.

DECORATE YOUR FIREPLACE

A fireplace can be a great focal point in a living room. Start by creating an anchor with a unique piece. A framed mirror works well, but if you have a sunburst mirror, or something with a unique shape, go for it! I am notorious for constantly switching the main focal point of my mantel each season. It's a great way to introduce the new seasons.

Next, add a collection or pairing of items. The mantel is a great place to showcase your collections of mercury glass, vintage pitchers, or any other beautiful objects. Have fun and express your personality with the pieces you select.

Add some height to offset the main focal piece. This can be candlesticks, a beautiful figurine, or even wall sconces flanked on each side. Think of a triangle when placing items, with your main focal point in the middle and your next highest pieces to each side.

Add some greenery or florals to your mantel for a natural organic element. It will add a touch of texture and life to your space. I love to use faux florals and greenery so I don't have to worry about changing the water, and my arrangements last longer.

MY FAVORITE ITEMS TO DECORATE A MANTEL

* Mirrors

* Art reflecting nature or the ocean

* Mercury glass candlesticks

* Ginger jars

* Blue and white vases and jars

* Sea glass bottles

* Faux florals: hydrangeas, cherry blossoms, peonies, tulips, lavender

BLISSFUL TIPS

Hang curtains high to make the ceiling appear higher.

Use console tables as a desk or TV stand to save space.

PLACE A RUG

I'm often asked how to place a rug in a room and how to choose the right size. This can be tough, but following a few simple steps will help you place your rug perfectly in any living room or space.

Typically, I like my rug 6 to 8 feet wider than the pieces of furniture that will sit on top of it. If the room size is not large enough to accommodate this, then it will look best with the front legs of all pieces of furniture resting on the rug. The size of the room will determine what is possible. Typically, I use an 8 by 10-foot or 9 by 12-foot area rug.

Since I am such a visual person, I use painter's tape to mark out the size of the rug on the floor. That way I can see the scale of it in the room and determine whether I need to go up or down a size.

Layering rugs can be a fun way to add color and texture to your space. When I do this, I usually use a 5 by 7-foot rug on top of an 8 by 10-foot rug. I like the bottom rug to be a jute, sisal, or tone-on-tone color, then I place a more patterned and colorful rug on top to add a pop.

MIX AND MATCH PILLOWS

Throw pillows can add a lot of personality and color to a living room. When choosing your pillows, the first step is to decide how many you'll need. I always start with four: two on each side of the sofa. The larger the sofa gets, the more pillows you'll need. My mantra is you can never have enough pillows, and I have baskets in my living room where I throw extra ones for when they are needed.

Typically, I use a 22- to 24-inch pillow for my back pillow, then go down in size as I move to the middle of my sofa. For instance, the ones next to the 22-inch ones are generally 18 to 20 inches. When buying pillow inserts, go up in size. When I have a 20-inch pillow cover, I purchase a 22-inch insert so my pillow looks nice and full. I love down or down alternative inserts and I often buy pillows, throw out the inserts that they come with, and put mine in. Sadly, relatively affordable pillows tend to skimp on the insert quality (hence their price), and replacing the insert is an easy way to elevate the look of the pillow.

As a general rule of thumb when mixing and matching pillow patterns, choose a main fabric either in a floral or multicolor pattern as your base fabric. To complement the base fabric, select a textured or geometric pattern or stripe in a large-scale print, then another textured or geometric pattern or stripe in a small-scale print.

How to Decorate a Coffee Table

Decorating a coffee table can be such a personal thing. I love to add little treasures that I've found and like to look at and use.

STEP 1 **Start with storage.**

This is where a lot of people need to store their TV remotes and other small items. I usually start with a catchall tray and build from there. This tray houses my remotes, coasters, and other utilitarian items that need to be corralled.

STEP 2 **Add books.**

Next, I love to add coffee table books. My favorites are books on art, the ocean/beach, European coastal areas, and, of course, interior design books, but you should choose whatever inspires you. These should be books you'll enjoy looking at often. Think of adding height with your books, so put out at least three, or two thicker books will do the trick.

STEP 3 **Bring in nature.**

Once the books are in place, add in a natural element like florals or greenery. This could also be something like a bowl of sea glass or wooden beads. Something that comes from nature is always a must.

STEP 4 **Add some height.**

Some believe that in order to create height, you have to add a tall vase or candlesticks. That's not necessarily true. Don't get me wrong—I love candlesticks on a coffee table— but they're not your only option. You can create height by adding an element on top of your stack of hardcover books, or even by stacking candles on a tray. Aim to create three levels of height: high, medium, and low. By placing some items directly on the table and others on books, you can create height without any tall pieces.

STEP 5 **Highlight your personality.**

Don't forget to add some of your personality or personal pieces, too. I have a little bowl on my coffee table with photographs of our family in it. We love to look at them when we are watching TV, and I update the photos often. You can also include pieces from your travels that you love to look at. Be creative and have fun!

Cabinet and Bookshelf Styling

ITEMS YOU WILL NEED:

* Paint or wallpaper
* New cabinet hardware
* Baskets
* Labels
* Books
* Whimsical decorative objects like bookends, spheres, or moss balls
* Vases
* Candles
* Sentimental items

Steps to refresh the look of your cabinet or bookshelf:

1. To update the look of your piece, repaint it, apply wallpaper, or replace the hardware.

2. Once you're happy with the look of the empty shelving unit, decide what you want to store inside any cabinets or drawers and what you'd like to leave out on the shelves as decoration.

3. Organize your items by category.

4. Use baskets in the closed portion of your cabinet to organize objects like picture albums, video games, puzzles, etc.

5. Add labels to these baskets and bins so it's easy to locate items inside.

6. Organize your books by theme or color.

7. Place the books on the shelves in groups to create a balanced look throughout.

8. Between the books, intersperse whimsical decorative objects like moss balls, seashells, and vases.

9. Finish off the shelves with candles and sentimental keepsakes to add personality and warmth.

3

Kitchen

The kitchen is the center of everyday life for many families, including mine. No matter how big or small your kitchen may be, you can create a warm, inviting space that works smoothly, feels inviting, and keeps your family happy and fed.

W HEN I THINK of the heart of my home, I always think of the kitchen. Our family uses this space for cooking, eating, homework, and just hanging out at the counter because it's the center of our open concept kitchen/living room area. It's so easy to pull up a barstool and sit at the counter, look at mail, and just nibble and chitchat with each other. I think of the kitchen as a place to reconnect and recover with your family after a long day.

So many memories are made in this space, too: teaching my daughter to boil water and make a mean grilled cheese, and sitting at the counter with my husband having a glass of wine, just talking about our day. It's funny—even in our tiny home in California, our kitchen was easily the smallest room, yet we still found ourselves in there more often than not. I had my family over for Christmas dinner one year, and there were seven of us huddled at a little table in the corner of the attached breakfast room. We would squeeze by each other to refill our plates, and there was just something cozy about it all. Those are the memories that live with me forever.

In this chapter, we'll work on making your kitchen the heart of your home and a blissful spot to unwind from the day with your family.

QUESTIONS TO CONSIDER BEFORE YOU BEGIN

* Where do you keep your utensils?

* How do you unload your dishwasher?

* Where do you keep your plates and glasses?

* Do you have space for cooking utensils in drawers, or can they be stored in a canister on the counter?

* Do you have small children and need dedicated cabinet space for their things?

* Do you cook a lot and have lots of bowls, pots and pans, baking sheets, etc.?

* Where will you place large kitchen appliances, such as a toaster, food processor, or coffee machine? Can some of these go in cabinets when they're not in use?

Purpose

Your kitchen's functionality is so important and should be the first thing you think of before you start decorating. You will be frazzled and feel disorganized when you are in your kitchen if it is not laid out properly, or if your drawers are not organized according to your family's needs.

One of the first things I do on a design consult for a kitchen space is to ask my client to walk me through how they would prepare a meal, or even just boil water. This tells me a lot about how they navigate the space and what elements they use most often. Even asking yourself how you wash your dishes and put them away is key to understanding a kitchen's flow. This will tell you where you will need to place utensils, pots and pans, dishes, glasses, etc. Ideally, everything should be placed close to where you would be using it in your kitchen.

Plan

Once I know how the flow of a kitchen needs to work, I plan out how to use different sections of the cabinet spaces and figure out how to organize everything.

SORT EVERYTHING

I create stations like baking, cooking, everyday linens, and a command center, which is a place to keep all your organizational tools like a calendar, pens, scissors, and notepads. Pull everything out of your cabinets and group them into these different stations, adding any that make sense to you based on your kitchen's flow. Gather anything else you think you will want stored in the kitchen and make sure your plan includes a spot for everything—if you find utensils or other kitchen items that you no longer use, toss or donate these. You may determine that you need more

or less drawer space for these different stations. This will help you decide whether you need to pare down or relocate some items somewhere else, like the pantry.

BASIC KITCHEN DESIGN STEPS

1. Decide what stations you need to create.

2. Declutter your kitchen utensils—what don't you need or use?

3. Plan out what storage equipment you'll need to purchase, such as utensil canisters, drawer dividers, bins, and so on.

4. Group similar items in piles.

5. Corral items neatly in cabinets with your storage equipment.

6. Label items to find them easily.

BLISSFUL TIP

Add color with accessories. Use faux florals, vases, and candles to add a pop of color.

STORE EVERYTHING

Once you've sorted all your items into the stations you're planning to create, it's time to put everything in its place. Figure out what storage pieces you need to house all your items neatly. I love to use drawer dividers, utensil trays, lazy Susans, and risers to fill up cabinet space better. Use labels so you can easily identify items in cabinets if they are in canisters, baskets, or bins. You will be amazed at how these extra organizational steps will make working in your kitchen such a breeze!

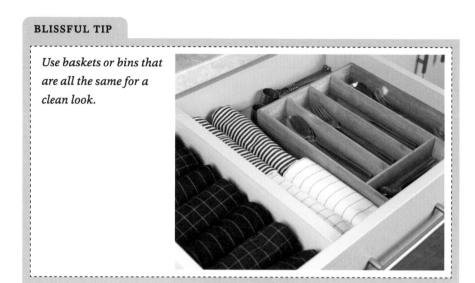

Use baskets or bins that are all the same for a clean look.

Decorate

No matter what the current trends are, you can create a classic, timeless kitchen that never goes out of style with a few tried-and-true tips. There are some key spots to address when you start to decorate to make your decor flow and not look cluttered or inconsistent.

SELECT HARDWARE

For many years, the trend was for all hardware and lighting finishes to match. In my opinion, that made everything a little boring and too monochromatic. I love mixing and matching finishes for a more eclectic look. But there is definitely a logic to follow when choosing which fixtures *do* need to match.

When selecting hardware and finishes, all hardware on the cabinets should either match the faucet or the lighting. For example, if you have gold lighting, then you can do gold hardware on the cabinets. But if you have black iron lighting and a chrome faucet, then you can't do gold hardware. Your hardware would need to be either chrome or black.

LIGHT YOUR SPACE

Let's talk about lighting! When it comes to finishes, use the same rule as above for hardware and either have your lighting match the cabinet hardware or the faucet finish. This simple trick will make your kitchen feel cohesive.

When picking a fixture to hang over a kitchen island, make sure to hang it above eye level so it doesn't obstruct your view. Normally there should be 30 to 36 inches between the top of the kitchen island and the bottom of the light fixture.

When it comes to style, I love glass pendants for smaller kitchens, to make them feel open and not so heavy, while a larger kitchen can take a more substantial fixture.

Have some fun selecting lighting—it's like picking jewelry for your outfit!

DECORATE SHELVES

If you have open shelving in your kitchen, that's the place to show off your beautiful china and any fun kitchen accessories you've collected. The biggest challenge is to make it look eclectic without becoming cluttered.

First, group similar items together: put bowls together in a stack, group glasses by size, and so on. These are the first items I put up on the shelves, and I spread them out so they are not bunched up together. If you have the space, give each of these categories its own shelf.

Next, add cookbooks to the shelves. Place two cookbooks under a stack of small plates to add height. Stack a few vertically next to the glasses, like bookends. Make these accessible so you can actually use them. Put the ones you use more often toward the bottom of your shelves so you can reach them.

Add small pots of herbs or plants to give your shelves some life. I love using faux plants so I don't have to remember to water anything. I am notorious for not having a green thumb!

I also love to add vintage baking pieces, like old rolling pins or antique ironstone pitchers. I feel old pieces bring warmth and a lived-in feel to the decor. You don't need many of these items, but even in a more modern space, antique wood tones and vintage pieces will transform it and make it feel less cold.

STYLE A COFFEE BAR

First, pick the space for your coffee bar. Do you have a stretch of counter space you can use? You can create the perfect coffee bar with just a small area designated for your items. Use a tray to hold everything, or place a shelf above your coffee maker to add space. Maybe you have a little extra space in a cabinet—use it to store your coffee maker for a hidden coffee station. Still not enough room? Use a rolling cart instead. Place it near a plug, and your coffee maker has a dedicated spot!

A useful coffee bar needs to be stocked with all the essentials. Here is my go-to list:

- » Coffee maker
- » Selection of coffee beans and/or K-cups
- » Coffee grinder
- » Coffee cups
- » Spoons
- » Napkins
- » Sugar and sugar bowl
- » Creamer
- » Cinnamon
- » Biscotti or other little tea crackers
- » Tray
- » Bowls/canisters for storage

Decorate and add your special touch to your coffee bar. Be it monogrammed napkins or a cute framed quote, your personal flair will make it feel all your own. This might be one of the most used spaces in our kitchen. My husband and I love to have coffee in the morning or before we start a movie at night. If you don't drink coffee, think about creating this for tea, or add in tea items to make a station for both tea and coffee.

SET UP YOUR COMMAND CENTER

A command center in the kitchen is the most efficient way to handle all your incoming mail and other items. The first step is to find a good spot. Maybe you have a small drawer or cabinet space, or maybe you just have a little spot on your counter. When I think of the flow of items coming in, I think you need to create three categories: items that need action, items that need to be kept or stored, and items to be filed.

The items that need action would ideally be dealt with as soon as you got them, but you may be running late for an appointment or have to get the kids off to sports. This would be your drop zone for the mail that needs to get looked at later or papers from school that need your attention.

The items that are kept or stored in the command center are things that should be accessible quickly when needed. These could be doctor's notes, Wi-Fi passwords, and emergency contact information. Just think of these as the things you want at your fingertips.

The items that need to be filed would go into your long-term filing cabinet system. Typically, I suggest filing everything on a biweekly or monthly basis, so the command center holds these items until you get to them. This would include paid bills, documents from school, and anything else you store and keep track of on a yearly basis.

Once you have items designated for these three spaces, you can see what storage/filing containers you will need. Use baskets, clipboards, or accordion folders. Placing a calendar here is a really useful way for the whole family to keep track of their daily/weekly schedules.

I love to have pens, pencils, scissors, and other small desk essentials handy here, too. Designate a junk drawer nearby for these items.

Having a system in place will save you lots of headaches and time for your busy family. If there is not a good place in the kitchen for a command center, then you can set one up in virtually any room, wherever it makes sense to you. Wherever you place it, the command center is a must-have.

MUST-HAVE, TIMELESS PIECES TO DECORATE KITCHEN COUNTERS

* Cluster of cutting boards

* Canisters for flour, sugar, and oats

* Beautiful soap dispenser

* Faux greenery in pots

* Candles

* Bowl with fruit

* Canister for utensils by the stove

* Cookbooks

* Beautiful pendant lights

* Tea towels

How to Make Stovetop Potpourri

I love a beautiful scent in the kitchen to evoke happy memories of gathering with friends and family and eating together. One of the ways I do this is with stovetop potpourri. It is so easy to make, and it's fun to get creative with different ingredients. I use a stovetop potpourri during the holidays, when I am entertaining, or just to refresh my kitchen. You can leave it in a pot on your stove for a few days, or store the mixture in a mason jar in the refrigerator to preserve it for a little bit longer. These also make great hostess or housewarming gifts!

STEP 1 **Gather your ingredients.**

Choose any good-smelling ingredients you have on hand—these are some great combinations:

* Lemon slices, rosemary, and vanilla, mixed with fresh thyme or mint

* Lavender, orange slices, and fresh thyme

* Apple slices, orange slices, cloves, and cinnamon sticks

* Lime slices, ginger slices, fresh mint, and fresh thyme

STEP 2 **Bring to a boil.**

Place all ingredients in a pot on the stove with a few cups of water. Turn the heat up to high and bring to a boil.

STEP 3 **Simmer and enjoy.**

Once the pot is boiling, reduce the heat to a simmer and you're done! Leave it simmering for as long as you want, but I typically simmer for 30 minutes to an hour, which is enough time to create a lovely aroma in the room. You can place the ingredients back in the fridge for a few days and reheat whenever you want.

Stocking Your Pantry

ITEMS YOU WILL NEED:

* Baskets
* Can riser
* Lazy Susan
* Food storage containers
* Bins
* Labels

STAPLE ITEMS TO KEEP IN YOUR PANTRY:

Canned goods
☐ Tomatoes
☐ Corn
☐ Green beans
☐ Refried beans
☐ Soups
☐ Pickles
☐ Red peppers
☐ Canned chicken or tuna
☐ Fruit

Cooking liquids
☐ Vegetable oil
☐ Olive oil
☐ Avocado oil
☐ Canola oil
☐ Cooking spray
☐ Apple cider vinegar
☐ Balsamic vinegar
☐ White vinegar
☐ Cooking wine

Vegetables
☐ Onions
☐ Potatoes
☐ Garlic

Snack items
☐ Trail mix
☐ Granola bars
☐ Energy bars
☐ Nuts
☐ Crackers

Packaged goods
☐ Cereal
☐ Muffin mix
☐ Cake mix
☐ Chips
☐ Macaroni and cheese
☐ Microwave popcorn
☐ Instant oatmeal
☐ Pasta and rice
☐ Bread

Sauces and condiments
☐ Ketchup
☐ Mayonnaise
☐ Mustard
☐ Salad dressing
☐ Tomato sauce
☐ Soy sauce
☐ Worcestershire sauce
☐ Teriyaki sauce
☐ Peanut butter
☐ Salsa
☐ Dried spices

Baking
☐ Flour
☐ Granulated sugar
☐ Brown sugar
☐ Powdered sugar
☐ Baking soda
☐ Baking powder
☐ Vanilla extract
☐ Corn syrup
☐ Cornstarch
☐ Oatmeal
☐ Yeast
☐ Baking chocolate

Storage and cooking aids
☐ Aluminum foil
☐ Wax paper
☐ Plastic wrap
☐ Plastic baggies

4

Dining Spaces

Your dining room table will be the setting for a lifetime of memories with family and friends. Set the scene for joyful mealtimes with a thoughtfully decorated and comfortable dining space.

Whether it's a full dining room, a breakfast nook, or just part of your kitchen, the dining space where you gather to share a meal is a particularly special part of your home. What's most important is creating a place where you can come together with family and friends and share stories and laughter around the table. In our family, dinner is truly the most special time of day: I love hearing about everyone's day and reconnecting after the time we spent apart.

In your dining space, you can surround yourself with thrifted items or the dining room set your grandparents had—mixing and matching is what makes the space full of personality! All the elements should work together in harmony to create a place where it's easy to make memories with your loved ones.

Purpose

Are you planning to use this area as a full dining room, a breakfast space, or both? It's helpful to think over how you'll be using the space every day, but also plan for special occasions. For example, if this room will be both a breakfast space and a dining room, then you'll want to keep some extra seating available for the times when you have visitors over for a meal.

On the other hand, if you have space for two separate eating areas, you can make the breakfast room chairs less formal (and if there are small kids in the house, easy to wipe down). Always prioritize making a room functional before you worry about making it pretty.

QUESTIONS TO CONSIDER BEFORE YOU BEGIN

* Do you have multiple eating areas, and if so, what will this one be used for?

* Who will be using this space every day?

* Will kids be using this space?

* Who might be using this space on special occasions?

* Do you need to have extra seating available?

* Does this space need to be multipurpose? Will it also be used for things like homework, a mini office, or crafting?

Plan

Keep your purpose in mind as you begin to plan the space: consider how many people you'll need to fit at the table on a regular day, and during any special events, and choose furniture with that in mind.

MEASURE FIRST

I always measure my space before I buy a bunch of stuff to start decorating. The worst thing you can do is get a table that is too big or just too small for what you need. Measure the whole room, then account for any other pieces of furniture that might go along the walls. Typically you want to leave at least 3 feet between the table and any other furniture or walls to be able to comfortably walk around your dining space. If you are in a smaller space, usually a round or an oval table is easiest to get around.

CHOOSE YOUR CHAIRS

Decide how many chairs you need. I love to have four chairs that are the same and then two chairs that function like captain's chairs at each end of the table, which can be upholstered or just a different style than the others. In a breakfast room, it can be great to use a bench instead of multiple chairs, especially for families with children. It is so much easier since more kids can squeeze in.

BLISSFUL TIP

Mix and match your chairs. Make an eclectic display with a variety of chairs. Or keep symmetry with two matching captain's chairs, and make the other four different.

If you are renting or can't change the color of your walls, bring a pop of color and dress up the space with window treatments. Don't let the color of the walls hold you back. Pick drapery that can tie it all together and make the space feel fresh and new.

CREATE AN ENERGIZING SPACE

Once you've thought through the table and chairs, come up with your color scheme and imagine the overall look of your dining space. Did you know the color red makes you passionate and energized? A lot of restaurants use this color to evoke emotion and make people excited to eat. This doesn't mean *you* need to go paint your dining room or breakfast room red, but when you are picking colors, think about how they make you feel. You want to be happy, upbeat, and excited to eat and sit with family and friends in this space, so use colors that give you that overall feeling.

Decorate

When decorating the dining room, there are specific items where I think a splurge is worthwhile, and others where it makes sense to save. I love affordable finds, and I've even gotten fancy dishes for a steal. You don't need a huge budget to bring a lot of personality to your dining space with creative centerpieces and table settings.

MAKE A BEAUTIFUL CENTERPIECE

I love a beautiful centerpiece on any table, even if it's just the breakfast room. The number one rule is to never make it so tall that you can't see the person on the other side of the table. Try a simple floral arrangement or a cluster of candlesticks, or both! Really, there is no right or wrong here. If I'm having brunch with the girls, I use citrus accents and a eucalyptus garland. This is so easy to do: just slice a few lemons and oranges and then cluster whole ones up and down the center of the table. In my breakfast room, my everyday centerpiece is just a simple bowl of fruit that my family can pull from to eat throughout the week. It is bright and colorful *and* feeds my family, which is a total win!

Use faux and real flowers mixed together for an affordable floral centerpiece that looks full and showstopping.

MY FAVORITE THINGS TO CREATE A BEAUTIFUL CENTERPIECE

* Flowers, both real and faux
* Mercury glass candlesticks
* Citrus fruits like lemons, oranges, and limes

* Eucalyptus garland
* White or clear vases
* Candles, both votive and pillar
* White dishes

GET CREATIVE WITH TABLE SETTINGS

Setting your table is a great place to get creative in your design. Throw caution to the wind, and have some fun! I have a full set (eight place settings) of plain white china that I use every day and as a foundation for my more elaborate table settings for holidays and special occasions. You can get plain white china just about anywhere, and it's such a good basic item to have on hand.

When a special occasion rolls around and I need to jazz up my table, I break out my smaller collections of patterned dinnerware. I love to layer my dinnerware with different patterns and colors for a unique and vibrant display. I have a small collection of cloth dinner napkins in various colors and patterns to add to the effect. Sometimes I put them under the flatware, or I will spice it up and layer the napkins on top of my dinner plates and under my salad plates. Changing out your plates and napkins and recombining them is a simple way to brighten your table for any occasion.

BLISSFUL TIP

Mix and match your china. I typically use white dinnerware because it goes with everything! Then I look for fun bowls, salad plates, and chargers that give me that wow factor. It makes my table more eclectic and less matchy-matchy.

How to Set a Table

For a more formal dinner or every day, follow these steps to create a gorgeous table.

STEP 1 Gather all the items you will need.

Gather your plates, chargers, silverware, glasses, napkins, tablecloth, and anything else you will use to set and decorate your table. Here is a list of the things I use, but you can customize depending on the occasion:

* Dinner plate
* Salad plate
* Charger
* Soup bowl
* Bread plate
* Butter knife
* Salad fork
* Dinner fork
* Knife
* Spoon

* Dessert fork
* Coffee spoon
* Coffee cup and saucer
* Red wine glass
* White wine glass
* Water glass
* Dinner napkins

STEP 2 **Lay down your linens.**

This can include your tablecloth, place mats, and/or a table runner.

STEP 3 **Place your chargers, plates, and bowls.**

For a formal dinner, I like to use a charger under my dinner plates, and sometimes I double up and use a pretty place mat under the charger. Depending on how you've set it up, you'll lay your plate down on top of the charger, on top of the place mat, or directly on top of the tablecloth. You may also add a soup bowl, bread plate, and stemware, depending on what you are serving.

STEP 4 **Lay down your napkins.**

Traditionally, a napkin is folded and placed to the left of the dinner plate. I love to mix things up from time to time, though, and use it to decorate the center of my plate. I either have it folded on top of my dinner plate, just under the dinner plate, or on top of my dinner plate under the salad plate or a bowl. There is no right or wrong way to do this, so have some fun!

STEP 5 **Place your flatware.**

Less-formal dinners have one fork, one knife, and one spoon. For a more formal dinner, you will need to use some additional pieces like a salad fork, butter knife, and dessert spoon. The salad fork goes on the outside of the dinner fork to the left of your plate. The knife goes on the right side of your plate with the sharp part of the knife facing toward the plate. The spoon rests next to the knife; lay the dessert spoon and fork above the top edge of your plate for a more formal place setting.

STEP 6 **Decorate!**

Now, add fresh flowers, candles, and other pretty little pieces to bring some pizzazz to the center of your table. I often group candles or add some small bud vases with flowers. Again, be creative and have some fun!

Dinner Party Planning

ITEMS YOU WILL NEED:

* Invitations
* Centerpieces
* Tablecloths
* Serving dishes
* Candles
* Food and drink items

Steps to Plan a Dinner Party:

1. Decide on your guest list. Typically, a good small gathering consists of no more than 10 to 15 people, and can be much smaller.

2. Select a date and time for your dinner party—make sure you're leaving yourself enough time to prepare!

3. Select a theme and color palette. For example, for a fall-themed party you could use warm earth tones and natural items as decoration.

4. Select your menu and plan your grocery list. Be sure your menu harmonizes with your theme, and check with guests for any dietary restrictions.

5. Create a music playlist that will set the right tone for the evening—it shouldn't be anything that would distract from conversation.

6. Plan your table settings and clean the dishes you're planning to use. This is a great time to bring out your more festive settings.

7. Designate a place where guests can leave their coats and other items.

8. Go grocery shopping to get all the food and drink items you'll need.

9. Shortly before the party, buy or create floral arrangements for centerpieces—make sure these will stay fresh until the time of the party.

10. Prep food before guests arrive—it's ideal if there are some things you can prep the day before, so you'll have enough time on the day of.

11. Set and decorate the table and get the lighting and music ready.

12. Plan to have all the cooking and decoration done 20 minutes before guests arrive.

5

Bedrooms

This is your space to decompress, unplug, and release the cares of the day. Your bedroom should be a sanctuary, and great design can transform it into the cozy, lovely nest you deserve.

Y OUR BEDROOM is an oasis of serenity, relaxation, and downtime, yet it's usually the last room in the house that gets decorated. I think that's because we're usually the only ones to see it, and it's generally behind closed doors. But because of its purpose, it should be one of the first rooms you tackle.

My husband and I have worked up to owning nice bedroom furniture, and our first "nice" bed came from a client of mine. We were redoing her bedroom and she had this beautiful wood sleigh bed she was getting rid of. I told her we slept on a mattress on a bed frame and she should sell or donate the bed. Well, lucky me, she donated it to us! We had that bed until just recently, for most of our married life, and I will always remember how grown-up I felt finally having a beautiful bed in our bedroom.

My point is, your furniture—even your bed—does not need to cost an arm and a leg. Your furniture can be hand-me-down, found in thrift stores, or purchased at a discount store. That's where I found my daughter Lauren's beautiful nailhead headboard for less than $150. The most important thing is how you pull all the pieces together and make them feel cohesive in the space.

Purpose

When I think back to our little home in Los Angeles, determining the purpose of the three bedrooms we had was simple. There was one for us, one for the baby, and one used as an office. Sometimes, when you have fewer choices, it's easier to design and decorate a space. My clients tell me that is one of the biggest challenges they face when decorating their homes—which is why they hire me.

QUESTIONS TO CONSIDER BEFORE YOU BEGIN

* Who is the bedroom for?

* Does it have closet space for everything you need to store, or will you need extra storage?

* Do you need additional lighting?

* Do you need desk space?

Upcycle furniture pieces found at garage sales and online marketplaces with a fresh coat of paint and new hardware. It's amazing how something as simple as paint can completely transform a piece.

If you are blessed to have an extra bedroom beyond the ones for you and the members of your family, then a guest room or an office space is so nice to have. I'll be honest: I think I have more fun decorating our guest room than our master bedroom! It's fun to play around with bedding and pillows, transitioning it through the seasons.

Determining who is using each of the bedrooms is definitely key, and the first step before beginning to decorate. If there is a teen using the bedroom, then they may want a place to do homework and use a computer. They may need a memo board to hang work or important notes. If the room is a nursery, you may need space for a changing table and rocking chair, or other essentials to make parenting tasks easier in this space.

Plan

Once you know who will be using the bedroom and what features you'll need to include, you can get into the details of planning the space.

CHOOSE A BED

Generally speaking, the bed is the focal point in any bedroom, so I love to look for a showstopper headboard. I'm drawn to details like nailheads, tufting, and canopies, but you should seek out a bed that fits into your design style and the overall look you are going for. I personally feel the place to invest is in a good mattress. This can make or break a great night's sleep and it's where you will spend most of your time in the room. Mattress preferences vary a ton, so go to stores and test them out!

BLISSFUL TIPS

If you have a small bedroom, add a large mirror to bounce light into the room from the windows, making it appear larger and brighter.

Use faux flowers and greenery to brighten the space and add warmth. This is also a great way to add a pop of color.

PLAN FOR STORAGE

Think about any storage issues you may need to overcome. Is there a large enough closet for the person who is going to use the room, or do you need furniture pieces big enough to store what doesn't fit in the closet? Decide whether you need baskets or other storage containers to make a tidy and easy-to-use closet space. I also love to plan what is going in each dresser drawer and select organizers for those as well.

SELECT LIGHTING

Is there enough lighting in the room? If you love to read in bed, then you should plan for some bedside lighting. When you're tight on space, swing-arm sconces are a good option. If you have the space on your nightstand, then beautiful table lamps can be a functional way to add dimension and height next to the side of the bed. You may want extra lighting next to any seating spots in the room. Upstairs bedrooms may deal with heat issues during the summer, and you may need a ceiling fan to help with your energy bill. I don't always love ceiling fans, but there are some nice options if you need one.

EXPLORE COLORS

Once I've planned out the furniture, I get inspired and start selecting colors and imagining the overall look and style of the room. Search Pinterest, websites, and magazines to collect ideas for what you want the room to look like. Do you want it soft and subtle? Then look for colors found in the ocean, like shades of blue and green. If you want it to be farmhouse style, then use neutral colors like taupe, white, black, and shades of brown. Use the "Bedroom Paint Color Guide by Style" sidebar to help navigate you in the right direction!

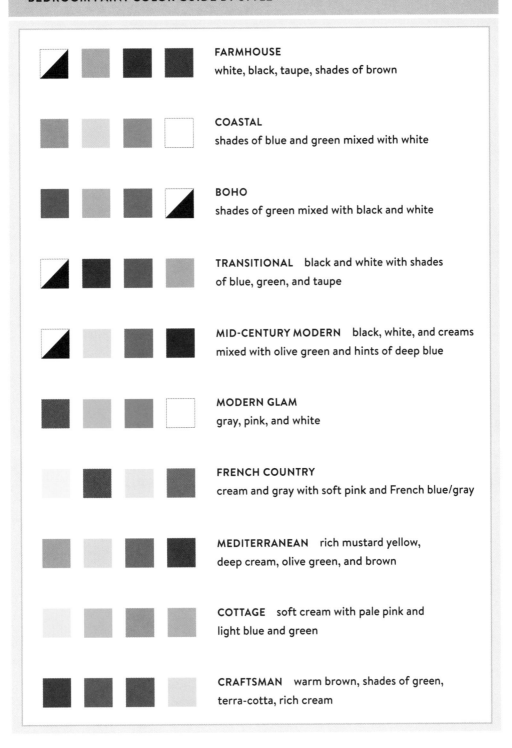

FARMHOUSE
white, black, taupe, shades of brown

COASTAL
shades of blue and green mixed with white

BOHO
shades of green mixed with black and white

TRANSITIONAL   black and white with shades
of blue, green, and taupe

MID-CENTURY MODERN   black, white, and creams
mixed with olive green and hints of deep blue

MODERN GLAM
gray, pink, and white

FRENCH COUNTRY
cream and gray with soft pink and French blue/gray

MEDITERRANEAN   rich mustard yellow,
deep cream, olive green, and brown

COTTAGE   soft cream with pale pink and
light blue and green

CRAFTSMAN   warm brown, shades of green,
terra-cotta, rich cream

Decorate

When decorating, focus on making your bedroom warm and relaxing—it should feel like a cozy sanctuary.

CHOOSE BEDDING

The best bedding is 100 percent cotton or linen. These fabrics are breathable and will last longer, through many washings. Be sure to check out my shopping guide at the back of this book (see page 154) for my favorite stores. Use my essential bedding checklist to shop for all the items you need to make the coziest bed!

When shopping for bedding, l love to mix and match. I pair my euro pillowcases with the duvet cover and the standard pillowcases with the quilt. This makes the bed look less matchy-matchy and more personal and pulled together. I add throw pillows in stripes and fun patterns in the same colors to lend a whimsical touch.

ESSENTIAL BEDDING ITEMS

* Euro pillows and pillowcases

* Standard pillows and pillowcases

* Flat and fitted sheets

* Two duvet inserts

* Two duvet covers

* Quilt or coverlet

* Throw blanket

* Mattress pad cover

* Bed skirt

COUNT YOUR PILLOWS

If you asked my husband how many pillows you need for a bed, he would tell you he just needs two to sleep on. Believe it or not, though, there is a certain logic to how many pillows to add to a bed. All of it depends on the size of the bed, as you'll see in the guide below:

Twin Bed

1 euro pillow
1 standard or sleeping pillow
Layer in accent pillows
    as desired

Full Bed

2 euro pillows
2 standard or sleeping pillows
2 accent pillows or
    1 long bolster pillow

Queen Bed

2 or 3 euro pillows
2 standard or sleeping pillows
2 or 3 accent pillows and/or
    1 long bolster pillow

King Bed

3 euro pillows
2 king-size sleeping pillows
2 or 3 accent pillows and/or
    1 long bolster pillow

PLAN A READING CORNER

I love to read, and my favorite place to do it is in the bedroom. I feel so relaxed and cozy in my bedroom, and I appreciate having a dedicated reading nook. Back in our small home in Los Angeles, we didn't have space for a reading corner, so I decorated my side of the bed with essential items for when I was reading: a table lamp, a jar of bookmarks, glasses, and fresh flowers. Now that we have a large bedroom, I was able to create a corner just for this sole purpose.

Pick a spot that's out of the way of too much traffic. It should feel like the most comfortable place in the bedroom, besides the bed. Some people choose a spot at the foot of their bed. If there is room near a window, you can have glorious sunlight streaming in while you read.

Once you choose your spot, start with cozy, soft chairs and a small accent table in between them. If you have a large space, then a small settee or sofa is such a nice luxury here. I like to have a little stool, bench, or pouf available to prop my feet up or even use as a small table. You can add a tray for extra surface space if you need it.

Next, stock the space with the essential items you will use. Here is a small list of things that I love to have:

- » Books
- » Throw blanket
- » Candle and matches
- » Throw pillow
- » Reading glasses
- » Small vase of fresh flowers

CREATE A GUEST ROOM OASIS

There are certain things I like to provide in my guest bedroom that I don't typically have in the other bedrooms. The goal is to create a private oasis for your friends and family when they come and stay, and they might be embarrassed to ask for things and not want to put you out. Having those items already there for their use just makes your guests more comfortable in the end. So here are the essential items that I like to place in my guest room and guest bathroom:

- » Extra blankets
- » A picture frame with the Wi-Fi password displayed
- » A carafe of water or bottled water and a glass
- » Extra sleeping pillows
- » A candle with matches
- » Magazines
- » Lots of freshly laundered guest towels (some people use more than one bath towel)
- » A jar or tray with extra travel essentials like a toothbrush, toothpaste, aspirin, lint brush, disposable razor, shampoo, and conditioner

How to Make a Layered, Cozy Bed

STEP 1 **Begin with the fitted sheet.**

The first step is to cover your mattress with a freshly laundered fitted sheet. I prefer fitted sheets with deep pockets so they're snug and fit fully over the edge of the mattress. Typically, I like to use white sheets because they look crisp, are easy to clean with bleach, and go with every bedding set. Fluff them in the dryer for 10 minutes with a damp cloth thrown in to get them wrinkle-free and crisp. Add some wool dryer balls with a little lemongrass essential oil on them.

STEP 2 **Lay the flat sheet.**

Lay the flat sheet on the bed upside down and pull it as far up to the top of the bed as you can. Then when you fold it over the duvet, you will see the pretty edge of the sheet. Fold in the ends at the bottom of the bed under the mattress. For an extra finish, you can press your sheets if they are still wrinkled from the dryer. I like to use a hand steamer to press out the wrinkles once the bed is made.

STEP 3 **Lay a duvet over the flat sheet.**

The next piece of bedding I add is a duvet on top of the flat sheet. I typically use a plain white duvet cover for the duvet fill, or simply layer another flat sheet on top of the duvet. During warmer months, I switch and use a lightweight coverlet, which can be cooler than a duvet.

STEP 4 **Layer a second duvet at the end of the bed.**

This is my biggest trick for making a bed look full and fluffy: add a second duvet to the bed. This is when I like to use patterned bedding to add color and visual impact. Fold over the second duvet a third of the way from the top to expose and show the underside. This is especially fun when the back has a different pattern. Make sure when you fold it over the end of the bed that it falls below the mattress and covers the end of the other duvet.

STEP 5 **Add a coverlet loosely across the middle.**

The next step is to add a coverlet to the middle section of the bed. This is another designer trick to making a bed look full and cozy. I gather the coverlet together loosely and drape it over the middle section of the bed, right on top of the exposed portion of the first duvet and over a little bit of the second duvet. During the winter, guests love having the option of multiple blankets on their bed.

STEP 6 **Add euro pillows.**

Add coordinating euro pillows to the back of the headboard that match the duvet at the end of the bed. This pulls the design of the bedding through and adds more pattern. For a king- or queen-size bed, use three euro pillows. For a twin-size bed, use one to two pillows.

STEP 7 Layer in standard pillows.

This is where I layer in my standard-size sleeping pillows. Because I use all white sheets, they fit perfectly into any bed color scheme and pillow combos. I place them right in front of the euro pillows—fluff them really well before you lay them down.

STEP 8 Add decorative pillows.

I love to add a stripe or smaller print that ties the bed color scheme together. On a king- or queen-size bed, I use two or three pillows here, and then one throw pillow in the front. Have fun with this, because this is where you can add some personality.

STEP 9 Add a throw blanket.

The last thing I add is a lightweight throw blanket. Placing this at the end of the bed makes it easy to grab and curl up in a reading chair or pull it over you while lying in bed. Sometimes I even keep a little basket in the corner of the room with a few extra throw blankets rolled up.

BEDROOMS

Closet Declutter

ITEMS YOU WILL NEED:

* Space-saving hangers
* Multi-hanging hangers
* Space-saving bags
* Baskets

* Bins
* Shoe risers
* Clear bins with lids
* Labels

Steps to organize your closet:

1. Set up three stations for keep, toss, and donate.

2. Start with one side of your closet and work your way around, removing each piece and placing it into one of the three stations. Do this for all hanging pieces, drawers, and shelves.

3. Wipe down all surfaces, dust all rods, and vacuum the closet.

4. Box up or bag all items to be donated and set them by the door to go out.

5. Discard everything to be tossed.

6. Determine sections for your closet for tops, pants, sweaters, shorts/skirts, shoes, and any other category.

7. Start sorting your keep pile into the categories you just set up and group together:

   * Tees
   * Tanks
   * Long-sleeve shirts
   * Sweaters and cardigans
   * Shorts
   * Pants
   * Skirts
   * Dresses
   * Blazers
   * Jackets
   * Coats
   * Shoes: sandals
   * Shoes: sneakers
   * Shoes: high heels/dress shoes
   * Shoes: boots/booties

8. Organize each category by color. Keep blacks together, blues together, etc.

9. Determine what should be hung, what can be folded, what isn't used often, and so on. This helps determine where to place your most-used items so you can easily get to them.

10. If you have a small closet, remove off-season clothing and fold and store it in bins. Bins can go under your bed or up high in your closet.

11. Set a declutter schedule to regularly purge your closet.

6

Bathrooms

- - - - - - - - - - - - - - - - - - - -

A beautifully decorated bathroom can be
a refreshing oasis, a place you come to
relax and rejuvenate. With some simple
updates, you can make your bathroom
both functional and fabulous.

DON'T KNOW ABOUT YOU, but I've always dreamed of a spa-like bathroom where I could just soak in a tub with candles and soft music playing in the background. When we lived in Los Angeles, we only had one bathroom in the whole house. It was only Bryan and I, and Lauren was just a baby, but even then it was so hard to shut myself in there for a soak when I knew someone might need something in the bathroom. What I did to make up for it was to add a few of my favorite things, like a yummy candle and some baskets to hold everything, to make me feel like I had a little part of what I was yearning for in a bathroom.

Even with the smallest bathroom, you can still attain a beautiful, functional space, no matter how many people are using it. We can't all have five bathrooms for every person in our home, but you can create a bathroom that has organization and beauty so when you walk in you instantly take a long, deep breath and relax.

Purpose

The essential purpose of a bathroom is very straightforward: it's where you take baths and showers and get ready for the day (especially if you don't have a walk-in closet). But the details can vary—a kid's bathroom, a guest bathroom, and a master bathroom all have different kinds of people using them, with different needs.

QUESTIONS TO CONSIDER BEFORE YOU BEGIN

* Who is going to use this bathroom?

* Do you take baths, showers, or both?

* Do you have a designated linen closet for this bathroom?

* Will medicine and first aid supplies need to be stored here?

* Will linens, towels, and toiletries need a home here?

* Will kids' bath toys need a spot?

Mount shower curtains as high as you can. This will make the room feel bigger and taller. Just measure carefully before mounting the rod and purchasing a curtain.

Guest bathrooms need basic essentials, just enough for guests to feel like they are at home and have things they need and might have forgotten on their travels. Kids' bathrooms may need more storage for things like bath toys, towels, and toiletries that adults typically don't use. So, first and foremost, ask yourself who is going to be using this space, and what needs they might have.

I always ask my clients to tell me how they get ready in the morning. Who gets up first and uses the shower? Who uses more of the things in the linen closet? Are some of the kids' things stored in the master bathroom? It may sound odd to ask these questions of someone you don't know very well, but I have found in all my years designing that function is the most important thing to address in a space. Form—which is all the beautiful accessories and decor—comes second.

Bathrooms are often fairly small, so understanding how they'll be used helps you prioritize storage and organization in a way that can maximize the space.

Plan

When I was a little girl, I dreamed of having a vanity space in my bathroom with all my makeup brushes and perfumes displayed perfectly. I wanted to always have fresh flowers in a vase and mirrored picture frames of my loved ones on the counter. Fast-forward to today: I live in a beautiful home, but there is no way I was able to design a bathroom with a special vanity area like this. What I *have* done is designate little spots for my items on the counter and organize my drawers and linen cabinet in a way that I like. My priority is to make sure I organize the bathroom so it reflects the way my husband and I use the space.

TAKE MEASUREMENTS

Measure your drawers, cabinets, and shelves in your linen closets. This will help when you are shopping for containers and drawer organizers and will save you money, too! I don't know about you, but I am notorious for buying cute baskets and bins that turn out not to fit when I get them home.

SELECT COLORS

Look at pictures, websites, and magazine pages for color schemes that inspire you. I bet you'll see a pattern. Use this to select the color palette you would like to use. Decide whether you want to apply wallpaper or paint the walls. Ask yourself whether these choices can work with the existing tile and materials in the bathroom, or whether you need to replace those things and create a whole new concept.

When you are selecting the colors for your bathroom, think spa colors. They are light and bright and soothing to your eyes, and you will look and feel refreshed when you're surrounded by them. Dark colors will feel heavy and absorb light. You will need a lot more lighting in the space if you use dark colors.

BLISSFUL TIP

Swap out builder-grade mirrors and replace them with inexpensive decorative ones to add style to the room.

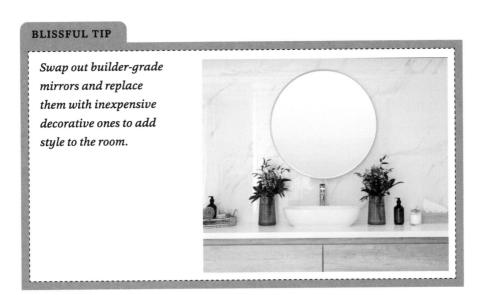

PLAN STORAGE SOLUTIONS

Create groups or categories of items that you use in the bathroom, and note where in the bathroom you usually use them, such as at the sink or in the bathtub or shower. This will help you decide where to store and house them. Keep bath salts and candles close to the tub and toilet paper not far from the toilet. If the linen closet is too far away, then use a pretty container near the toilet for toilet paper.

Plan where to store all your medicines, linens, makeup, and other supplies, so they'll be easily accessible when you need them. Think about whether you need drawer organizers to separate hairbrushes, toothpaste, and makeup. Start building your shopping list for all the storage solutions you need for your drawers and cabinets to help fit things neatly.

Decorate

Now comes the fun part! Bathrooms can (and should!) be as beautiful as they are functional.

LOOK AT LIGHTING

You can never have enough lighting in a bathroom. I can't begin to tell you how important it is to have the best lighting possible. It's not enough to have two sconces on either side of a mirror. Having recessed overhead lighting and a pretty chandelier add to the overall illumination of the space. Put each of the lights on different switches so you don't have them on all at once. Trust me, you definitely don't want low lighting when you are trying to put on your makeup.

Use clear containers in your linen closet so you can see everything you have. This will help you avoid accidentally buying too much of something when you think you're out.

FIND FUN CONTAINERS

I love to shop! One of my favorite things is to find pieces I can use in a variety of ways, like small containers, vases, and apothecary jars. Of course, I get the drawer organizers and baskets, too, for clear and easy storage. But for your counter, where things will be sitting out in plain view, you can have fun with containers.

I like using simple, modern-looking trays or large plates to corral all my little vases and jars on the counter. These make the counter look less cluttered and more organized.

GET GUEST BATHROOM ESSENTIALS

I always have a few essential items on hand in the guest bathroom for when visitors may have forgotten something. I collect little travel-size samples like soaps, shampoos, and hairspray, and place them in an apothecary jar in my guest bathroom. I always think it's nice to have them there and easily accessible so guests don't feel embarrassed asking for something. I also provide a hair dryer and place shampoo, conditioner, and a small variety of body washes in the shower. I also usually have a few loofahs on hand so they can use one and throw it away after their stay.

How to Make Mojito Sugar Scrub

I love to make a batch of my mojito sugar scrub for guests and place it in the guest bathroom as a little gift. Everyone loves how delicious it smells and asks for the recipe, so I thought I would share it with you, too!

INGREDIENTS

½ cup sugar

½ cup fractionated coconut oil

¼ teaspoon vitamin E oil

15 drops lime essential oil

10 drops peppermint essential oil

STEP 1 **Make the scrub.**

Pour the sugar into a bowl. Add the fractionated coconut oil, vitamin E oil, and lime and peppermint essential oils. Mix well. Store the mixture in an airtight container for up to 6 months.

STEP 2 **Use the scrub.**

While you're in the shower, rub a small amount of the mixture into your skin and then wash it off with warm water.

Linen Closet Organization

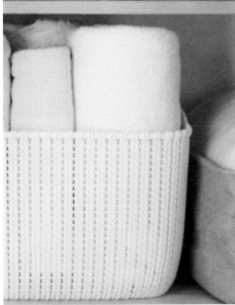

ITEMS YOU WILL NEED:

* Baskets
* Bins
* Clear boxes
  with lids
* Space-saving bags
* Lazy Susan
* Door organizer
* Labels

Steps to organize your linen closet:

1. Remove all items from your closet and sort into keep, toss, and donate piles.

2. Wipe down all shelving and vacuum.

3. Sort items to keep into categories:
   - Towels: bath, hand, washcloths
   - Sheets
   - Blankets
   - Medicine
   - First aid supplies
   - Lotions
   - Vitamins
   - Toilet paper
   - Hair tools/accessories
   - Beauty supplies

4. Designate placement on shelves for each category.

5. Fold and group items into containers for maximum storage space.

6. Arrange towels and bedding by size once folded.

7. Stack storage containers to get maximum use of space.

8. Add labels to all storage containers.

7

Office

If you're planning to do much work at home, it's essential to have a dedicated space where you can focus. Planning a well-designed office is about more than just organization, though—it's about making a peaceful place where it's possible to plan, create, and get things done.

A HOME OFFICE is a room where you can dream, plan, and create. I look at my office as my sanctuary, where I can think about where I want my business to go and what I currently have on my plate. It's where I come up with my best ideas and then execute them. My husband sometimes pops his head in for a quick chat when I'm working and my daughter Lauren will sprawl out with her coloring books on the floor on the odd day she is home from school when I'm working. I see this room as my place to let creativity flow and build plans.

I feel it is so important to have a workspace, whether you're in a little apartment, a rental house, or your dream home. We all need a dedicated spot where we can get tasks done, small or large.

As our lives change over the years, so does our workspace, and we need it to be able to grow with us. My guide will help you plan, organize, and use your office space to the fullest!

Purpose

Many new homes are built with a small home office space, but if you live in an older home, you may have to carve out an area for a little nook or take over an unused guest room. Regardless of the size of your home, everyone needs a small office space.

QUESTIONS TO CONSIDER BEFORE YOU BEGIN

* Where in your home is your office space?

* Do you work from home?

* How much storage space do you need?

* What space will you need to dedicate to electronic equipment, like computers, screens, and printers?

* Do you need additional lighting?

* How many people are going to use this space?

In our home in California, we did not have the luxury of dedicating a whole room as an office. Our third bedroom was a storage room, since we had absolutely no closet space and the smallest garage you've ever seen. So I added a desk and chair to our little living room and it was perfect. I had a view of my backyard—the outdoors inspires me and I could watch my little one play while I was working. Now that we have moved and have an actual dedicated office, the real luxury is having more storage for everything I need in order to run my at-home business.

It's worth thinking about how much you will use an office space before you take over an entire room. If you just need to open mail and write bills, then maybe that extra room could be turned into a craft space or a playroom. If you run your own business from home, then you'll definitely need the storage, so taking over a guest room might be worthwhile. Before you decide where to place your office, think carefully about what spaces you have available and what exactly you'll need the office area for.

Plan

No matter what space you have, as long as it's well organized and you have the right pieces, you can create a great office space. Creating a workspace that works for you is of the utmost importance. This will make you more successful at completing the tasks at hand.

WRANGLING ELECTRONICS

When planning your space, think through where to place your computer, printer, and any other office tech pieces that are cumbersome and need an outlet. It's ideal to have these pieces accessible but not seen. If possible, I hide them in a cabinet with a hole cut into the back so I can pull the wires through. This is a great way to hide all those wires. I also keep a basket or other storage piece next to my desk for wires, to help tidy up the tangled mess they can create. I use zip ties to help separate them and keep it all clean.

STORING PAPERWORK

Think about what kind of storage you need for all your paperwork. Where will it all go? Do you have a closet that you can use, or would a bookcase be a good place to put all your office essentials? The best way for me to determine this is to declutter and organize all my paperwork into piles at the beginning. This helps me see everything and figure out what organization pieces I can get to house it all.

Create a seating space with a cozy chair and an ottoman for a reading nook.

PLAN TO SHARE

These days, so many couples both work from home, so it's very common to plan an office that both can use. This can lead to space issues—it's hard to accommodate two desks and have enough storage space—so you'll want to take this into consideration when planning the room. Think about what each person's needs will be, and plan out how to set aside dedicated space.

If you're lucky enough to have the space, it's ideal if you can designate different office areas for each person working from home. My husband actually uses the fourth bedroom as his office. He usually goes in to work, but he loves being able to have a space at home where he can go and close the door for some work time as needed.

PLACE THE LIGHTING

Think about whether you will need some task lighting to read or do other work at your desk. Place your desk in a spot where you'll have room for a light source as well as all your other electronic equipment. If you're likely to have a lot of virtual meetings, then avoid placing your desk with your back to the window, because that will make your face appear shadowed. Think about adding a light source that will illuminate your face while you're onscreen.

Decorate

Once you have your space planned out and have decided how to use it, then you can begin decorating! Decorating your office is so much fun and should get your creative juices flowing—think about what decor will make you calm and productive.

CHOOSE YOUR COLORS

When thinking about the color scheme, I start with an area rug. It sets the tone for a room and then you can pick furniture colors, window treatments, and upholstered furniture without it all clashing. Because I am a creative, I like a more neutral-colored space. This helps my brain focus on colors for my clients and not drift to other spots in my office. This is a little trick I picked up early in my design career, and it has always made great sense to me. For analytical types, having a vibrant color palette might make you feel more productive. Some of my favorite colors for an office are white, navy blue, light gray, and sage green.

Add pops of color to your office with decor, faux florals, drapery, and throw pillows.

SELECT FURNITURE

After finalizing the rug and colors, I select the desk and any accent furniture. Since I need more surface space to spread things out, I picked a desk with a large top. I have a rather small office, so I tucked my desk up next to a wall to make it easier to get around. I also went for a wood-toned desk to add warmth to the space. Remember, avoid having three different wood tones in one space when choosing furniture. It will clash and look mismatched.

ENHANCE YOUR SHELVES

The closet attached to my office space is small, so I opted for some bookshelves. I picked some beautiful and inexpensive cabinets from Ikea and personalized them with removable wallpaper in the back. It added a hint of pattern and gave the shelves a more built-in, modern look. This little trick will make your decor pop.

PICK BEAUTIFUL LIGHTING

Task lighting is a must for an office desk—it's both functional and beautiful. Table lamps can make a room feel so inviting and illuminate your workspace to help you see better. They can add height as well as texture and color. A table lamp is one of those decor pieces I use in almost every room of a home, because it helps add a cozy vibe to a space.

KEEP IT FRUGAL

I love to shop for office items at affordable stores, since bookshelves and storage pieces can get pretty pricey. Also, thrift stores, flea markets, and secondhand shops are gold mines. I love looking for pieces that have a little history that I can either paint or just clean up. This is a great way to get more bang for your buck and not break the bank.

ESSENTIAL OFFICE ITEMS

* Desk

* Bookcase or storage piece

* Comfortable desk chair

* Table lamp

* Baskets for additional storage

* Organization containers

* Area rug

* Window treatments

* Chandelier or main light fixture

How to Declutter

It's vital to have an office that's neat and organized, so you can have everything you need right at your fingertips. Follow this process to declutter your office or any other space.

STEP 1 Schedule a block of time to focus on decluttering.

Organizing and straightening up your space takes time. I like to block out at least an hour of time per area I'm going to work on.

STEP 2 Keep only what you've used in the last year.

Let go of the idea that "maybe I could use this item in the future." Nope! That pack rat mentality isn't going to work if you want to make your office clutter-free. If you haven't used an item in the last year, it needs to go in a trash bag or donation pile unless it's an important document.

STEP 3 Get rid of duplicate items.

If you have multiples of one item (unless we're talking light bulbs and batteries), then the extras need to go. This is especially true when it comes to decluttering and organizing your closets and drawers. Trust me, you do not need five staplers.

STEP 4 Create a designated spot for everything you want to keep.

Everything needs a home. Use clever container ideas for drawer organization to help you maximize your storage space. I use cute boxes, trays, and even repurposed tissue boxes to help me stack items in cabinets (and to organize tough areas).

STEP 5 **Utilize your furniture storage.**

Do you have a desk with storage or an empty bookcase? You'll be surprised by how much more space you create in these spots when you have the right containers to store your items.

STEP 6 **Label every item.**

Making labels may seem like a time-consuming process, but it's well worth the effort when you see the finished result stacked in your neat storage areas. Even if you can't see into the box or inside the back of a dark cabinet, you still know what items are in there.

STEP 7 **Cut back on paper clutter by digitizing your keepsakes.**

Do you have tons of photos? It might be time to store most of them on your computer (or in cloud storage). It's a little frightening to part with those treasured items, but once you see how much it cuts back on paper clutter, you'll be convinced. I store my photos both on my computer and in the cloud for safekeeping.

STEP 8 **Divide your remaining items into three piles.**

Once you've pared down your stuff, labeled, and designated a spot for each item you want to keep, you probably have a big pile of things to get rid of. Turn your "don't keep" pile into three categories: sell, donate, and trash.

For each item, first ask yourself whether you can sell it. With online selling options like Craigslist and eBay, and local consignment shops, you might earn a little extra money from items you aren't going to use anymore. For everything else, donate what's in decent repair, and trash the rest.

STEP 9 **Keep it up!**

Decluttering your office is just the first step. You need to incorporate organizing into your daily life. Adopt a new policy to return an item to its spot after you use it. Plan a regular decluttering session once every three to six months, to keep things from getting out of hand.

Essential Office Supplies

ITEMS EVERY OFFICE SHOULD HAVE:

Furniture:
- ☐ Desk
- ☐ Office chair or other seating
- ☐ File storage
- ☐ Bookshelf
- ☐ Task and overhead lighting

Organization:
- ☐ Baskets
- ☐ Clear bins
- ☐ File folders
- ☐ Pencil or pen tray
- ☐ Folders and binders
- ☐ Paper tray
- ☐ Drawer organizers
- ☐ Labels

Paper goods and stationery:
- ☐ Pens
- ☐ Pencils
- ☐ Highlighters or markers
- ☐ Printer paper
- ☐ Pads of paper
- ☐ Notebooks
- ☐ Sticky notes
- ☐ Envelopes
- ☐ Stamps

Electronics:
- ☐ Desktop or laptop computer
- ☐ Screen and screen riser (if necessary)
- ☐ Keyboard and mouse
- ☐ Headphones and/or external speakers
- ☐ Printer and scanner
- ☐ Chargers
- ☐ Surge protectors and items to corral power cords

Other supplies:
- ☐ Stapler and staples
- ☐ Tape dispenser and tape
- ☐ Glue
- ☐ Pencil sharpener
- ☐ Scissors
- ☐ Label maker
- ☐ Desk or wall calendar
- ☐ Trash bin

8

Children's Rooms

Decorating rooms for the youngest members of your family can be particularly fun! Bring some whimsy and personality to the project, and remember to create a space that can grow along with your little ones.

THE TIME SPENT preparing for your child to be born is incredibly special. There is absolutely nothing like it. I always wanted to be a mom, and originally wanted four children and a large family with lots of kids running around all the time. Fast-forward to the present day, and we have one sweet little girl. The funniest thing is that both my husband and I are only children and we ended up having only one child—it's funny how things work out like that.

Decorating Lauren's nursery was an absolute dream for me. It was pink with black and white touches. I had read that babies see black and white first, so I wanted that to be prominent in the room. I loved that beautiful little room in our tiny home in Los Angeles. To me, it was perfect.

Lauren is now thirteen years old and it has been quite a struggle for us to agree on a room design. She is a horse-obsessed girl who literally remembers where every stuffed animal has come from, its name, and its specific spot in her room. But we finally got to a place where I could translate what she loves into an elevated and modern space she can grow into as a teen.

With a little bit of guidance, you can find common ground with your kiddo when designing and decorating their room, no matter what age they are!

Purpose

Keep a few things in mind as you start designing this space. Think of what your child or preteen currently likes and what you think will fade away in the next few years. For instance, does your little one love Curious George or rainbows right now? You can use those color schemes to make a space that will feel sophisticated once the rainbows and monkeys are gone.

QUESTIONS TO CONSIDER BEFORE YOU BEGIN

* What theme/color scheme do you want?

* Do you need more storage in this room?

* Do you need a study space?

* What pieces of furniture do you want?

* Do you need additional lighting?

* How can you plan for this room to grow up with your child?

Next, think about how your child is going to use this room now and in the future. If they end up like most teens, at some point they will probably spend a lot of time holed up in there. Is there a place to do homework, and a seating area that's not the bed? I thought about this even when Lauren was seven! If you think and plan ahead like this, in the long run you are going to save lots of time and money on redecorating when they want something different in a few years.

Plan

Let's make a plan! It's wonderful to involve your child in the planning, but keep the options simple if you can. If you need to show your kiddo the design plans for the new room, then come up with just two room designs with the essential pieces and bedding to show them, no more. Kids have short attention spans, so when they're presented with too many choices, they will either want it all or not choose anything and say they hate everything. Less is more!

FIND INSPIRATION

I think visual collages are key not only for adults but for kids too. If you know how to use Photoshop or PicMonkey (or some collage-making website), then you can pull your selections into a collage. I literally do this for every single room I design (even for myself). I am such a visual person and this makes it really easy to see whether all the elements I'm choosing will work together.

BLISSFUL TIP

Use baskets to store stuffed animals, pillows, and extra throw blankets for the bed.

SELECT FURNITURE

When selecting furniture for kids' rooms, make sure you find pieces that will transition well as they grow up and withstand a lot of wear and tear. In general, a kid's room should be functional and split into four main sections: sleeping or resting, working or learning, storage, and play. Of course, as your child gets older, their needs will change—because of this, you might want to buy less expensive furniture for the storage and play zones.

Look at the sizing of the pieces you select. Will your child be able to reach what they need to reach or climb up on the bed easily? Look for well-made pieces that can take a beating and still look great. Strong chairs and easy, wipeable surfaces are key. Prioritize practicality and durability.

CHOOSE YOUR STYLE

As for the style of furniture and overall look of the room, I suggest selecting classic pieces. A simple bed frame or one upholstered in a cream or denim fabric will go with just about any color scheme. I tend to choose color palettes over an actual theme in a room to make it easier to transition into other themes later on. Kids change their minds so much, but if you choose colors they love, then the design of the room will last longer.

ASK YOUR CHILD THESE QUESTIONS:

* What are your favorite colors?

* What theme do you want the room to be?

* What do you like to do in your room besides sleep?

* Do you need book storage or toy storage?

* Do you need a homework spot?

* Do you need art storage?

* Where do you want to place trophies and sports items?

* Would you like and use a reading corner?

Store off-season clothing or clothing that's the next size up in storage containers under the bed to maximize space in the closet.

PLAN FOR STORAGE

Once you both have come to a final plan on the design, make a list of everything you will need. This is the time to start thinking about organization strategy for all those stuffed animals and artwork that keeps piling up. Think about how to maximize the storage in the closet and maybe even utilize the space under the bed. That's where I store Lauren's off-season clothes so they don't take up valuable space in her closet.

Here are a few things I pay particular attention to when planning storage in a child's room:

» Make sure you have lots of storage options like shelving, baskets, and drawers. Create a little system so that at the end of the day, everything gets put away.
» Add cube storage. This is fabulous for toys that need to be easily accessible but not seen. I love the pieces at Ikea for this. They are affordable and have so many options to choose from.
» Make sure storage is at eye level. If kids see it, they will use it. You don't want to buy all these amazing things for your kids that just get stacked high in the closet and never used.
» Use labels to help organize. This helps kids recognize where all their things go and encourages them to put everything away properly.

Decorate

It's so much fun to decorate a kid's room—you can get more whimsical and creative than you might in the adult spaces of your home.

PICK COLORS

Color schemes for kids aren't so gender-specific anymore, which I love. For example, my daughter loves blue. Everything has to be blue. So, we chose a color scheme of lilac and blue to create a very girly but not babyish space for her. Get as creative as you want with this process!

Here are some of my favorite color combos, but go with your child's preferences, whatever they might be.

SUGGESTED COLOR PAIRINGS

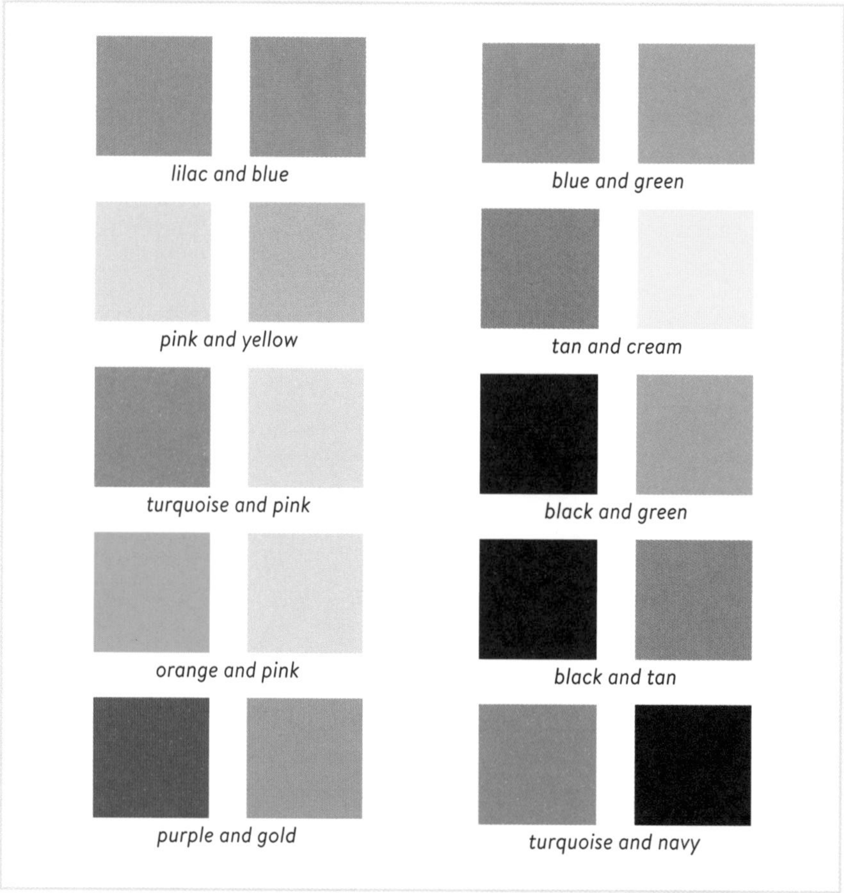

lilac and blue

blue and green

pink and yellow

tan and cream

turquoise and pink

black and green

orange and pink

black and tan

purple and gold

turquoise and navy

STORE KNICKKNACKS

Kids have a lot of little knickknacks and keepsakes. I use bookcases and shelves for these and group things that are similar, like trophies and awards all together, books stacked neatly on a shelf or two, and so on.

CHOOSE LIGHTING

It's great to place a table lamp next to the bed for reading before bed. I also like to put task lighting on a desk. Sometimes the beautiful chandelier we've picked out that looks amazing does not provide enough light for these little activities.

CREATE FUNCTIONAL DECORATIONS

Ideally, you can blend decorations with useful storage. For example, if your child likes to wear hair bows, use pretty ribbon from the craft store to make long strips, hang them on the wall, and attach the bows to them. This is a cute and inexpensive way to keep the hair bows neat and accessible.

How to Make Over a Nightstand

An inexpensive nightstand or side table from a thrift store or garage sale is an affordable solution for a child's room. Here is an easy way to update and refresh the piece!

MATERIALS

* Thrifted nightstand or side table
* Drop cloth
* Hand sander with 120-grit sanding disks
* Damp cloth
* Primer (optional)
* Chalk paint and paintbrush or spray chalk paint
* Chalk paint wax
* New hardware (e.g., knobs or pulls)

STEP 1 **Prep the piece of furniture and sand.**

Remove the hardware and any other pieces that you are replacing and lay the nightstand on a drop cloth. Then, using your sander and sandpaper, lightly sand the whole piece. Wipe down with a slightly damp cloth when done.

STEP 2 **Prime the piece of furniture (optional).**

If the piece is made of darker wood, then the furniture will need a primer. Apply per the instructions on the can and let it dry completely.

STEP 3 **Apply the first coat of chalk paint.**

Apply chalk paint with a paintbrush, or if you selected spray chalk paint, use long, even strokes to avoid drip marks. If you do see drip marks, just take a slightly damp cloth and smooth them out gently. Let the first coat of paint dry completely according to the can's directions.

STEP 4 **Apply the second coat of chalk paint.**

Add another layer of chalk paint evenly over the first. Let it dry completely. If you feel you still need another coat, then simply repeat this step.

STEP 5 **Apply a light coat of wax.**

Apply a coat of wax all over the fully dried painted surface. This will help improve the durability of the paint. Apply according to the instructions on the can.

STEP 6 **Replace the hardware.**

Add any new hardware and you are done!

Organize Children's Rooms and Closets

ITEMS YOU WILL NEED:

* Space-saving hangers
* Multi-hanging hangers
* Space-saving bags
* Baskets

* Bins
* Shoe risers
* Clear bins with lids
* Labels

Steps to organize children's rooms and closets:

1. Set up four stations for toss, keep in room, keep in storage, and donate.

2. Next, think about what you need to store in the room and in the closet. You can plan out areas to store the following categories of items:

   * Toys
   * Stuffed animals
   * Books
   * Arts and crafts supplies
   * Imagination corner

3. Start at one end of the room and work your way around the space, putting items in each of the four stations. The "keep in storage" station should be for things your child has outgrown that you still want to keep (or things they'll grow into soon) and the "keep in room" station should be things they currently need and use.

4. Work through the closet space in the same way, moving items to the four stations.

5. Discard or give away the items in the toss and donate piles.

6. Assess your storage needs for all the items remaining and decide where you want to put them. Add shelving, bookcases, etc. for bulk storage.

7. Wipe down all existing shelving and furniture and vacuum the space.

8. Organize the clothes in the closet by type (long sleeves, short sleeves, pants, sweaters, etc.) and group within each type by color.

9. Put all items in bins or other containers and put them in the spaces you've designated.

10. Label all bins and storage containers.

Outdoor Spaces

When the weather permits, it's lovely to have a comfortable outdoor space to enjoy. Set up attractive areas for cooking, eating, relaxing, or playing, and the possibilities for outdoor fun will be endless.

WHEN I REFLECT on our time living in Los Angeles, I think back to what our home was like there compared with where we are now and I realize how much our living habits have changed. Our first home in Los Angeles had a decent backyard with a covered patio area, a brick side patio, and a grass area with tall juniper trees to hide the view of the hotel on the other side of the fence. Though this was of course not ideal, we loved our little backyard. It was Lauren's place to play in the sandbox and the playhouse we built for her. We had her first birthday party there with fifty of our closest friends—I have no idea how we got everyone in our backyard!

The point is, no matter what your outdoor space is like, you can make it perfect for you. Bryan and I have lived in apartments, tiny houses, rentals, and now in our beautiful home. We have been through it all, and I have dealt with everything from no backyard to balconies, patios, and small side yards. You can spruce up any outdoor space and make it a sanctuary to enjoy.

Purpose

To start off designing an outdoor area, you have to look realistically at how much space you have to work with. There are some ideas, like an outdoor kitchen, that you'll likely need to scrap if you don't have much room. But you can definitely divide up even a small space to work for multiple purposes.

I love to have a cooking space for a barbecue and a dining area—for me, these are the two most important things. If you can add in a lounge space, that would probably be next. These answers might be different for you, though. Ask yourself what you would do outside most often, given the space you have, and plan accordingly.

QUESTIONS TO CONSIDER BEFORE YOU BEGIN

* How big is your backyard space and/or patio?

* Do you like to barbecue?

* Do you like to have outdoor get-togethers?

* Do you need to create privacy from neighbors?

* Do you need dining space outside?

* Do you want to create a play area for children, or any other recreational area?

Plan

Once you've figured out how you want to use the space, it's time to start planning for furniture and any other outdoor pieces you may want. To avoid buying anything you don't need, make a shopping list of the main pieces to look for before you go out.

USE RUGS TO DEFINE SPACES

I like to set the stage for different areas with outdoor area rugs. Boy, have these come a long way from ten years ago! There used to be very little to choose from and they were super hard and scratchy. Now, you can find them in just about any pattern or color you could ask for. I love to place one under lounge areas and dining spaces to define them more clearly, especially because these areas may be on the same patio.

CONSIDER OUTDOOR LIGHTING

Lighting is another outdoor decor piece that has come a long way in recent years. In the past, outdoor lights were typically boring flush-mount fixtures that had no character and were pretty ugly. Now you can get chandeliers, sconces, and even outdoor floor lamps to make your patio look and feel like an indoor space. Before you purchase lighting, think about your space, where you might need extra lighting, and what kind of mood you'd like to create.

BLISSFUL TIP

Patio spaces can sometimes be tight— when choosing furniture, remember that typical pass-through spaces should be 30 to 36 inches for people to comfortably walk around furniture.

MAKE A VIBRANT YARD

Is there planting you can do to help transform your yard into a more vibrant and luscious space? Maybe plan for a vegetable garden and map out where you would like it to go. When I plan my planters, I look for affordable, beautiful flowers that bring instant color but don't break the bank. My actual garden is where I spend a little more money and get quality year-round plants that will last.

A fireplace or firepit is great on a patio, but lanterns with candles can also make your outdoor oasis feel dreamy!

Decorate

There are some essential tricks to creating a beautiful, updated outdoor space. First, we'll focus on the patio, and then move on to the rest of the yard.

UPDATE THE SEATING

Patio furniture has morphed from metal chairs and vinyl cushions to beautiful woven sofas and chairs with soft cushions and fun throw pillows. There are so many great places to shop for affordable outdoor furniture, and some of my favorites are listed in the back of this book (see page 154). Look for pieces that not only fit the dimensions you need but are also comfortable and stylish. When you do pick your outdoor cushions and throw pillows, make sure they use outdoor fabric—it should be easy to keep clean and resistant to summer storms.

ADD THROW PILLOWS

I add new throw pillows every spring to instantly transform the look of my patio space—this can refresh your color scheme and give a fresh look to your patio setup. I look for pillows in outdoor fabrics and inserts that I know are weather resistant and can handle the extreme heat in the summer. Coordinate the colors with your area rugs to pull the look together.

REFRESH PLANTERS

I have a small collection of pots in my garage, but somehow, they always seem to get nicked every season. So, I like to buy fresh, new pots for our front porch and patio. I prefer simple, modern pots in white or gray. Vary the heights so you can group them together.

UPDATE OUTDOOR LIGHTING

Updating your sconces and other decorative outdoor lighting can change the whole look of your house. You can give your house a modern polish by selecting rectangular sconces, or choose lanterns for that farmhouse look. Another great way to highlight your home is to add up-lights in front of your windows in the flower beds. These flood your front windows with light at night and actually make the pitch of your roof look taller in the evening. Lastly, consider adding landscape lighting. These lights can illuminate a pathway on the edge of your garden and outline your flower beds. If you don't want to invest in electrical for them, there are solar-powered options that are just beautiful!

BLISSFUL TIPS

Painting or staining your front door will make it feel fresh and inviting, especially when it brings an unexpected pop of color! Black, navy blue, creamy white, or silver gray-blue can be great choices.

Seasonal wreaths are an inexpensive way to bring color and flowers to your porch. Add ribbon or extra flowers to fill out a store-bought wreath.

PLANT FLOWERS

Another reliable way to update your yard is by planting in-season blooms that give an instant pop of color and freshen up your curb appeal. Either line the garden's edge with seasonal flowers or add them to planters on your front porch. Check with your local nursery for the hardiest choices. This will depend on the season you're heading into—can the plants withstand the cold, or will the heat burn them? If you don't have a large enough space to plant flowers in the ground, then consider a cluster of pots on your front porch.

How to Keep Your Lawn Beautiful

Your outdoor space will look especially inviting if you follow these simple steps to keep your lawn healthy and beautiful.

STEP 1 **Aerate your lawn at least once a year.**

This will help with water drainage and nutrient absorption. There are a couple of tools you can use for this, like an aerator with a foot bar or one that fits on your shoes.

STEP 2 **Use lawn fertilizer.**

Lawn fertilizer will help your grass grow faster and keeps it fuller and greener. It will also help protect your grass from disease and make it more resilient.

STEP 3 **Water longer but infrequently.**

The best rule of thumb is to cut your grass long and then it will grow thicker roots. The longer the grass is, the less frequently you need to water it. Experts recommend watering 1 inch per week, which is 20 minutes three times a week, but check with your local nursery for your soil and climate.

Prep Your Yard for Spring

ITEMS YOU WILL NEED:

* Gardening gloves
* Rake
* Shovel
* Grass seed
* Fertilizer for flower beds
* Mulch
* Aerator
* Pruners (shears)
* Lawn mower
* Fertilizer for grass
* New plants and flowers
* Power washer or hose

Steps to prep your yard:

1. Clean all gardening tools and replace broken ones.

2. Rake dead leaves and garden debris from winter.

3. Reseed bare patches in your lawn.

4. Pull all weeds.

5. Fertilize garden beds.

6. Apply mulch to garden beds.

7. Aerate the lawn.

8. Prune bushes.

9. Mow lawn.

10. Fertilize the lawn after the first mow.

11. Plant new flowers in garden beds.

12. Plant new plants and flowers in containers on patio.

13. Power wash the patio.

14. Wash down patio furniture.

15. Clean cushions and pillows.

16. Fix fence if needed.

17. Reseal the fence if it has been more than two or three years.

Decorating with Trends

- - - - - - - - - - - - - - - - - - -

Redecorating a space according to a new design trend can be a great way to refresh the look of your home. With the tips in this chapter, you'll discover how to choose elements that are on-trend while retaining some timeless essentials.

A S A CHILD, I was notorious for going to flea markets with my parents, finding all kinds of new design styles, and falling in love with them. I would run back to my parents and try to convince them that my current bedroom was now out of style and I needed to buy these new treasures now or I would never find them again. I would get home and completely dismantle my room, rearrange the furniture for the hundredth time, and then put it all back together with my new finds. I went through an astrological look, Southwestern vibe, and the black-and-white mod look of the early 1990s, just to name a few. I was hooked on this inexpensive way of reinventing the hottest new trend.

My love for shaking things up in my home decor has never gone away. I jokingly tell people that when my husband comes home from work each night, he isn't sure he's in the right house.

Over many years of doing this work, beginning way back before I even went to design school, I developed tricks for keeping up with home decor trends without spending a lot of money.

Purpose

Ask yourself whether a trend you're eyeing is something you'll want to have in your home for a long time. Is this just fun for now, or do you really want to embrace this new look and stick with it for a while? It's important to think this through carefully—if you're just looking for a change of pace, try to find decor you can tweak later on to evolve into a different style, without having to scrap everything entirely.

If your space has a good basic design, adapting it to different styles is not that hard. For instance, if a room started out with a very rustic farmhouse

QUESTIONS TO CONSIDER BEFORE YOU BEGIN

* Do I have pieces in my home that already fit into this design trend?

* What is my budget for this makeover?

* What pieces can be thrifted?

* Are there pieces of furniture I have that can be easily transformed to this new style with a little DIY?

* What decor do I have that I can sell or purge?

look, with lots of chippy, painted pieces of furniture, slipcovered sofas, and vintage light fixtures with an overall white color palette, you could easily transition it into a new design style. You could make it more industrial looking with darker, moodier colors. You would look for lighting in metal finishes like black and silver. Decor accents would be in reclaimed wood and much more minimal looking. But the slipcovered sofas and vintage pieces could still work. For this reason, most of my designs start with neutral furniture pieces so they can work over time with different styles.

Plan

Once you have decided on a new design style, plan out how you'll transform your space.

DECIDE WHAT STAYS AND WHAT GOES

Study your new design style and take note of its key characteristics, focusing on colors, furniture styles, and materials like wood tones. This will help you decide what to keep and what to discard. Then begin purging your space. Do your main furniture pieces work with your new design style? As I mentioned above, most neutral furniture can work in just about any style, but patterns or bold colors could pose more of a challenge. Once you've tackled the large pieces, move on to smaller elements like coffee tables and side tables. Decide what can stay and what should go, then plan out how you'll arrange everything in the space (including any new pieces). Only once this is done should you move on to paint and color palette decisions. These give you the biggest style impact with the least amount of change and effort. Don't ever underestimate the power of paint!

PLAN YOUR BUDGET

Before you dive into shopping, plan your budget. I like to spend more on things I will have longer—timeless pieces and substantial furniture items. Back those out of your overall budget first. Then decide how much you can dedicate to lighting, paint, window treatments, throw pillows, and accent decor. Break this down into a spreadsheet for yourself and when you purchase things, compare the price to what you had in your budget column. You may end up spending less on something and be able to move the surplus to another item. This is how I decide whether I can buy that $100 pillow: if I can save somewhere else, I might be able to splurge on a more expensive item.

Decorate

My best trick to introducing new design trends to a space is to start from a foundation of furniture that does not lend itself to one particular style or another. Pick furniture that has clean lines, minimal details like tufting or nailheads, and a simple silhouette. This goes for all pieces, even coffee tables and side tables. Then you can introduce a new design style with accessories, paint, and area rugs.

ADD COLOR WITH FABRIC

Bring in color with fabrics in pillows and window treatments or go simple for a more modern look with creams, whites, and browns. Use throw pillows to really pop your design trend. Pick two or three pillow styles to use throughout your space: one should be in a small pattern, one in a texture like linen or a heavy-textured fabric, and one in a larger pattern or print. This helps create a more eclectic look. Then, use these three pillow styles on a sofa, side chair, or bench to spread out the color and patterns.

HOW TO MAKE A DECORATING BUDGET

1. Create a wish list of items.

2. Set your overall budget for the project.

3. Make your design plans for the space.

4. Compare prices of decor and get familiar with the price of goods.

5. Narrow down your wish list.

6. Prioritize your purchases.

7. Buy your top priorities first, and be sure to keep an eye on your budget throughout.

8. Have fun decorating!

BRING IN TEXTURE

Another great way to bring in flair from your new design style is to add texture with an area rug. This will give your design depth and lend some warmth. Don't be afraid to add a fun patterned print or colors on top of something more neutral like a jute rug. An area rug can really make your furniture stand out, especially if you have some neutral pieces. When you add an area rug, you are setting the stage for your room.

Shop at thrift stores, antique stores, and flea markets for vintage pieces in your chosen design style.

Choose furniture with relatively simple silhouettes so it can go with multiple design styles.

CHOOSE NEW LIGHTING

The next step is to choose new lighting. This is the easiest way to announce a room's style. Art deco and mid-century modern have very specific-looking lighting. Industrial and farmhouse styles use iron pieces that are more rustic. I start with the main light fixture for the room, like a chandelier. Focus first on finding the right metal finish, and then the silhouette. After you select a main lighting piece, move on to smaller accent lighting. Will

you need some ambient lighting like table lamps or wall sconces? Be sure to choose metal finishes that echo the main fixture you selected to bring cohesiveness to the room.

INTRODUCE ACCENT PIECES

Lastly, you can introduce larger accent pieces like side chairs, ottomans, benches, and side tables. These are not essential when trying to bring a new design style to your space, but if you can splurge, this is where you should do it. Tie pattern and color to the area rug and pillow selections with these pieces for a seamless look. Match wood tones to other major pieces of furniture in your room. Too many different wood tones in one space will make the pieces look out of place.

Furniture Guide by Style

Here's a quick introduction to some popular design trends. Take a look at these examples to get a sense of what appeals to you and matches your personal style.

FARMHOUSE The farmhouse design style is very rustic in nature. It uses a neutral color palette of cream, beige, earth tones, gray, tan, and brown. Furniture is in vintage antique finishes and reclaimed wood is used throughout the space. Light fixtures and hardware are in iron or galvanized finishes. Walls are painted white and/or covered in shiplap. Vintage accessories are key, and the focus is on a room feeling comfortable and timeworn.

COASTAL The coastal design style uses a very similar color palette to the farmhouse look, but focuses on a more modern aesthetic. Light, open, airy floor plans with weathered wood finishes and earth tones mixed with white on white are hallmarks of this design. And yes—lots of shades of blue reminiscent of the ocean. Furniture is meant to be casual, and straw, seagrass, and jute textures appear in area rugs, furniture pieces like barstools, and even throw pillows. When looking for lighting think of chrome, satin nickel, and black.

TRANSITIONAL If you are swaying between design styles, this might be the one for you. The transitional design trend is a mesh of modern and contemporary—simplicity and sophistication. The main colors are neutral, like white, gray, and tan, with darker colors as accents, such as brown, blue, green, and black. Most of the furniture pieces have a plush, comfortable look and float in the room (not up against walls). Pops of color appear in window treatment fabrics and small accessories like pillows and vases. Statement pieces, like tables, dressers, and mirrors, come from different eras. Lighting is usually contemporary fixtures in gold or bronze finishes.

BOHO The boho look is globally inspired. It is full of life and culture and features pieces that reflect nature. It is carefree, relaxed, and eclectic. The colors are warm and earthy: jewel tones, deep browns, shades of green, and gray as a base to ground the other colors. Ikat and dyed textiles as well as tapestries are very popular. A lot of natural elements like jute and sisal with vintage chenille are prevalent. The furniture looks like it has been collected over time and feels eclectic. This design style is also great for plant lovers! Lots and lots of plants are featured throughout, so usually these spaces have great natural light.

MID-CENTURY MODERN The mid-century modern design style has a Scandinavian influence with clean, simple lines in the furniture silhouettes and sleek wood like teak, rosewood, and walnut. This design style is not afraid to mix patterns and colors, but in a refined way that relies on accessories rather than major pieces of furniture. Saturated colors, such as blue, gold, rich brown, and green, are dominant. Art can take center stage in a room with this design style and can have a retro, funky look to it. Lighting fixtures feature gold or black finishes.

MODERN GLAM The modern glam look is traditional in its main decor pieces but has a lot of ornamental details with a bit of pizzazz. You'll see lots of layered neutrals mixed with a pop of bold color or pattern in shades of pink, black, white, gold, and gray. Furniture may have smooth glossy finishes, and nailhead-trimmed upholstery or a tufted sofa is a must! Lighting is dramatic, with crystal-adorned chandeliers, table lamps, and sconces.

FRENCH COUNTRY The French country style is an elevated look with a more rustic design base. This look features traditional furniture with more ornate wood details. Side tables and coffee tables may have some gold and glass accents. The colors are neutral in base, but work in soft blues, golds, and tans. Patterned area rugs with some color are prevalent and coordinate with the throw pillows and window treatments. Lighting and hardware feature antique brass, pewter, and polished nickel. Beautiful ornate mirrors, candlesticks, and vases are perfect accessories for this look.

11

Choosing Paint

Selecting just the right color for a room sets the tone and style for the entire space. With this guide, figure out how to choose the right paint color and finish to complement and enhance your decor.

OR SO MANY, choosing paint for a space is such a high-stress decision, and it can be really nerve-racking when you aren't sure what the final result will look like. The only way you can gain more confidence is to train your eye by looking at paint more carefully and observing how different settings and lighting affect it. After doing this hundreds of times for clients, I still don't always get it right. This is why putting samples up is so important! Follow these steps to make this process a little easier.

Guide to Choosing Paint

STEP 1 **Decide on a color.**

I know, easier said than done, but once you've picked the overall color you want, it's easier to start pinpointing specific shades to try out.

STEP 2 **Pick two to four shades of that color to try out.**

Even when you think you're looking at four samples of the same color, you'll notice different shades can be cool or warm. Cool colors tend to have more white in them and are more stark, where warm shades have more yellow in them. Neither choice is right or wrong. It will depend on your inside lighting, how the sun hits the house at different times of day, as well as the colors in the furniture you want to work with. Each of these will alter the color you see on that small sample in the store.

When you have picked the overall color you want, select one or two shades, both lighter and darker, to try out, for the reasons above. You just have no idea what they will end up looking like once they are up on the wall.

STEP 3 **Paint samples.**

This is the fun part, in my book—I love testing out wall colors. When you have picked two to four shades, grab a small quart of each from the paint store. If you already have dark walls, then put on a layer of primer before you paint on your samples, or else they won't reflect the true shade of the paint.

Paint your samples relatively large—I typically do about 24 inches square—and in multiple spots around the room. That way, I can see what each shade looks like facing the windows, in a dark spot, and with lights on.

Take your time picking the final shade of paint. Look at your samples during the day, at night, and with the lights on and off in the room. All these factors will change the color, and before you commit you want to make sure you love the shade in all these different circumstances. When you're sure, go ahead and get started on painting the room!

Guide to Paint Finishes

When selecting paint, you're choosing more than just color: you also need to decide what finish to pick. Each finish reflects a different amount of light off the painted surface. The more sheen, the glossier the paint finish. The finish also tells you the durability and washability of the paint. The more sheen a paint has, the easier it is to wipe down (like in a bathroom space) and it will be longer lasting than a matte paint. Below, I have broken down all the finish options you can choose from and what they work best for.

MATTE/FLAT

This finish is best for ceilings and low-traffic rooms. It isn't very reflective, so it's good for walls with blemishes, texture, or any other imperfections. It dries pretty quickly and can be difficult to clean.

EGGSHELL

This finish has slightly more luster to it than a flat finish, but does not look shiny. This is used in a wide variety of rooms, like living rooms, bedrooms, dining rooms, and offices. It can be wiped with a damp cloth to clean and doesn't get stained as easily as flat finish.

SATIN

Some people think satin and eggshell are the same. While they are similar for the most part, satin finish is slightly more reflective than eggshell, making it easier to wipe clean if needed. Typically, this is used in kids' rooms, kitchens, bathrooms, and game or playrooms.

SEMI-GLOSS

This finish has more sheen to it than an eggshell or satin finish and typically is used for trim. It is easy to clean and resists humidity, making it a great finish for bathrooms. Definitely use this paint in high-traffic areas that need to be wiped down a lot.

HIGH GLOSS

Typically, this is used on cabinetry and trim work. It is super easy to wipe clean, but less forgiving of any imperfections like holes or texture. It is the perfect finish if you want to use a dramatic color on a cabinet in a bathroom or kitchen for a striking contrast.

MY FAVORITE PAINT COLORS BY DESIGN STYLE

Over the years, I have had the pleasure of designing spaces in homes that have incorporated many different design styles. I have used paint colors that I know have great versatility and go with specific design looks. So I have put my favorite paint colors together by style for you to reference when you are ready to transform your next space.

FARMHOUSE

White Heron
(Benjamin Moore)

Classic Gray
(Sherwin Williams)

Sea Salt
(Sherwin Williams)

Wrought Iron
(Benjamin Moore)

COASTAL

  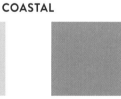

Chantilly Lace
(Benjamin Moore)

Topsail
(Sherwin Williams)

Santorini Blue
(Benjamin Moore)

Hale Navy
(Benjamin Moore)

TRANSITIONAL

Oxford White	Repose Gray	Solitude	Indigo Batik
(Benjamin Moore)	(Sherwin Williams)	(Benjamin Moore)	(Sherwin Williams)

MID-CENTURY MODERN

Oxford White	Shoji White	Repose Gray	Iron Ore
(Benjamin Moore)	(Sherwin Williams)	(Sherwin Williams)	(Sherwin Williams)

BOHO

Oxford White	Stonington Gray	Silver Sage	Iron Ore
(Benjamin Moore)	(Benjamin Moore)	(Benjamin Moore)	(Sherwin Williams)

MODERN GLAM

Chantilly Lace	Stonington Gray	Rose Silk	Pitch Black
(Benjamin Moore)	(Benjamin Moore)	(Benjamin Moore)	(Benjamin Moore)

FRENCH COUNTRY

Chantilly Lace	Repose Gray	Pink Bliss	Hinting Blue
(Benjamin Moore)	(Sherwin Williams)	(Benjamin Moore)	(Sherwin Williams)

Conclusion

HAVE ALWAYS WANTED a dream home, but for many years I did not know what that looked like. Through grit and determination as well as my experience working in the design industry, my home has evolved into a sanctuary for me and my family. It is nowhere near perfect, but it is the perfect place for us. The word *home* is defined differently by everyone. What makes the perfect home for you should and will look different than my perfect home or anyone else's.

There is so much beauty in the journey to achieving your home design goals, and I hope this book will help you. I want you to use this as a resource guide, and I want to champion you through the process. Use this book to find comfort and strength in your design decisions. Help define your style and how your family needs to function in the spaces you have in your home.

Of course, this is a process, and your design journey won't be complete overnight. It's actually just the opposite: your home will keep evolving, just as you do. The key is to base your design in classic roots that can adapt to the wave of trends over time. I hope you'll find that ability to adapt and grow through using this book and my three basic design steps: purpose, plan, and decorate.

Above all, remember your home is a personal expression of you and your family. It should be unique and represent you and your stage of life, whether you are newlyweds, new parents, or empty nesters. Function and form always need to work together. Life and design are both journeys, and my hope is for you to create a blissfully stylish home you'll love every step of the way!

My Favorite
Places to Shop

I am a shopper at heart. I love a good deal, I love the history of beautiful pieces, and I love to get the look for less! Over the years I have spent a lot of time shopping for others and have discovered some tried-and-true shopping resources that I keep going back to time and time again. So here is a list of my favorite places to shop and what I like to buy from them—an eclectic mix of high end and low end.

AFLORAL
The best for faux florals and greenery

AMAZON
Easy-to-find small decor pieces with fast shipping

ANNIE SELKE
Known for a wide selection of beautiful rugs

ANTHROPOLOGIE
Love their candle assortment

CAITLIN WILSON
Known for beautiful patterned pillows and gorgeous area rugs

EBAY
Expensive decor pieces for a fraction of the cost

ETSY
Great source for designer fabric pillows

FACEBOOK MARKETPLACE
Useful source for secondhand furniture

H&M HOME
Great place for affordable throw pillows

HAYNEEDLE
Huge furniture selection

IKEA
Perfect for filler furniture or rooms with lower budgets for bigger decor pieces

JOSS & MAIN
Designer-quality furniture selection

KIRKLANDS
Affordable farmhouse-style decor accents and furniture

LAUREN HASKELL DESIGNS
My go-to place for ginger jars

MCGEE & CO.
Lovely small decor accents like cutting boards, baskets, and vases

NORDSTROM
Love their assortment of throw blankets, candles, and serving pieces

POTTERY BARN
Quality furniture and my favorite for pillows and decor pieces

SERENA & LILY
Gorgeous furniture, but their pillows are my favorite

TARGET
Good accent decor pieces and small accessories

TERRAIN
Great gardening pots and small accent decor pieces

WALMART
Affordable and trendy decor like table lamps, trays, and organization pieces

WAYFAIR
Huge furniture selection

WILLIAMS SONOMA
The best for kitchen essentials and kitchen decor

WORLD MARKET
My go-to place for entertaining and kitchen decor pieces

Spring Cleaning Checklist

KITCHEN

- ☐ Clean counters, sink, and faucet
- ☐ Clean out cabinet under sink
- ☐ Deep clean garbage disposal
- ☐ Clean out refrigerator and shelves
- ☐ Vacuum under refrigerator
- ☐ Wipe down microwave
- ☐ Deep clean stove
- ☐ Deep clean dishwasher
- ☐ Clean out drawers and cabinets
- ☐ Wipe down cabinets
- ☐ Declutter and organize pantry
- ☐ Dust lighting fixtures
- ☐ Clean windows
- ☐ Take out trash
- ☐ Vacuum
- ☐ Mop

DINING ROOM

- ☐ Dust furniture
- ☐ Wash tablecloths
- ☐ Clean crystal and polish silver
- ☐ Clean curtains, windows, and blinds
- ☐ Shake out area rug and/or clean carpet
- ☐ Wipe down baseboards
- ☐ Vacuum
- ☐ Mop

LIVING ROOM

- ☐ Dust vents, baseboards, and light fixtures
- ☐ Clean curtains, windows, and blinds
- ☐ Shake out area rugs and clean carpets
- ☐ Dust furniture
- ☐ Dust knickknacks
- ☐ Dust picture frames
- ☐ Wash throw blankets
- ☐ Wash pillows
- ☐ Wipe down electronics
- ☐ Declutter cabinets
- ☐ Check smoke detector
- ☐ Wipe down baseboards
- ☐ Vacuum

BATHROOMS

- ☐ Wipe down counters, sink, and faucet
- ☐ Clean mirrors
- ☐ Dust lighting fixtures
- ☐ Clean out drawers and cabinets
- ☐ Clean out drains
- ☐ Scrub toilet
- ☐ Deep clean shower
- ☐ Wash shower curtain and bath mats
- ☐ Organize under sinks
- ☐ Take out trash
- ☐ Wipe down baseboards
- ☐ Sweep
- ☐ Mop

BEDROOMS

- ☐ Strip beds and wash bedding
- ☐ Flip and rotate mattress
- ☐ Dust vents, baseboards, and light fixtures
- ☐ Clean curtains, windows, and blinds
- ☐ Shake out area rug and clean carpet
- ☐ Dust furniture
- ☐ Dust knickknacks
- ☐ Purge closet and donate clothes
- ☐ Wipe down doors and light switches
- ☐ Check smoke detectors
- ☐ Wipe down baseboards
- ☐ Vacuum
- ☐ Mop

ENTRYWAY

- ☐ Clean out hall closet
- ☐ Clean up shoes and coats
- ☐ Dust furniture and knickknacks
- ☐ Shake out area rug
- ☐ Wipe down baseboards
- ☐ Check smoke detector
- ☐ Vacuum
- ☐ Mop

OFFICE

- ☐ Declutter and organize files
- ☐ Dust furniture
- ☐ Dust bookcase and shelving
- ☐ Shred old papers
- ☐ Organize desk drawers
- ☐ Declutter desktop
- ☐ Shake out area rug
- ☐ Wipe down baseboards
- ☐ Check smoke detector
- ☐ Vacuum

LAUNDRY ROOM

- ☐ Wipe down washer and dryer
- ☐ Run washer on sanitize cycle
- ☐ Clean lint trap
- ☐ Purge cabinets and organize cleaning supplies
- ☐ Throw out old cleaning cloths
- ☐ Wipe down baseboards
- ☐ Vacuum
- ☐ Mop

Acknowledgments

This book would not have been possible without the work and support of so many amazing people in my life. Everyone needs a village for support and companionship on life's journey, and I am so blessed and grateful for my village.

To Bryan, my amazing husband: I love you so much. You are my biggest supporter and just when I didn't think I could go back to school and get a design degree, you encouraged me to go. I would never have been on this journey if it wasn't for you. I am so lucky to have the most generous, kind, and loving person by my side.

To my sweet Lauren: You are my shining light and I am so incredibly blessed to be your momma. God gave me the greatest gift in you, and I could not be prouder of the beautiful, kind soul you are. I hope you know that you can always shoot for the stars because they are made to be grabbed. This book and my career came about because I wanted to be a mom and create a cozy nest for you and your daddy to enjoy. I hope you always know how much you are loved.

To my parents: I love you both more than you will ever know, and thank you for always supporting my dreams. I am so thankful you took me junking as a kid so I would grow up knowing and appreciating the "find"! Dad, I sure wish you could be here to enjoy this with me, but I know you are shining down bright from heaven.

To Audrie: I love you my dear friend and you inspire me on so many levels. I am so happy we created these images together and I could not have made this book without you. I love to dream BIG with you, girl!

To Tiffany: I am so grateful for you and your friendship. You have made me strive for more and push myself to do things I never thought I could do. This book would not have been possible without your guidance. You are such an amazing soul and I am so blessed that you walked into my life.

To Rage: Thank you so much for seeing the potential in me and taking a chance on me. I never thought I would have the opportunity to create a beautiful design book and I am so grateful.

To my Quarto family: You all have made my dreams come true! What a gorgeous book we have all made together, and all your hard work is present on every page. I am so grateful to Katie, Todd, and the rest of the team for keeping me on track and their constant professionalism and dedication. Thank you for helping me make a book that I am so proud of.

To my designer and blogger friends: Thank you for being some of my biggest cheerleaders, inspiring me and always being there when I needed you. Being surrounded by these exceptionally creative and hardworking people is such a blessing and pushes me to accomplish more.

To my readers: You are why I get to do what I love every day. Because of your support and love over the years we have built the most amazing community and I am so thankful for each and every one of you.

And thank you to God for being my guiding light in all things and giving me the most amazing life.

About the Author

REBEKAH DEMPSEY is an interior designer, creative director, and stylist, best known for her successful interior design site, A Blissful Nest. Before moving to Texas and starting her blog, Rebekah established herself as the senior designer of a well-known Los Angeles-based design firm. Rebekah's desire for every person to love their home the way she loves hers inspired her career of helping others learn how to turn their homes into havens. On her blog and social media, Rebekah shares her keen eye, design expertise, and wide-ranging knowledge of interior and exterior design trends. Rebekah currently lives in a small suburb of Dallas with her husband Bryan, daughter Lauren, and their dog, cat, and horse. Learn more about her home renovations and current decor projects at ABlissfulNest.com and find Rebekah on Instagram at @ABlissfulNest.

Rebekah has been recognized as a *Better Homes & Gardens* Stylemaker since 2015. Her work has been featured in *Better Homes & Gardens* and MarthaStewart.com, and she has collaborated with Home Depot, Behr, At Home Stores, KitchenAid, Serena & Lily, and HGTV.

Inspiring | Educating | Creating | Entertaining

Brimming with creative inspiration, how-to projects, and useful information to enrich your everyday life, Quarto Knows is a favorite destination for those pursuing their interests and passions. Visit our site and dig deeper with our books into your area of interest: Quarto Creates, Quarto Cooks, Quarto Homes, Quarto Lives, Quarto Drives, Quarto Explores, Quarto Gifts, or Quarto Kids.

First published in 2021 by Rock Point,
an imprint of The Quarto Group,
142 West 36th Street, 4th Floor,
New York, NY 10018, USA
T (212) 779-4972 F (212) 779-6058
www.QuartoKnows.com

Rock Point titles are also available at discount for retail, wholesale, promotional, and bulk purchase. For details, contact the Special Sales Manager by email at specialsales@quarto.com or by mail at The Quarto Group, Attn: Special Sales Manager, 100 Cummings Center Suite 265D, Beverly, MA 01915 USA.

10 9 8 7 6 5 4 3 2 1

ISBN: 978-1-63106-727-3

Publisher: Rage Kindelsperger
Creative Director: Laura Drew
Managing Editor: Cara Donaldson
Senior Editors: Katharine Moore and John Foster
Cover and Interior Design: Laura Shaw Design
Photography by Audrie Dollins, except the following: pages 20, 32 (top), 34 (bottom left), 37 (top), 46, 49 (top), 71 (top), 82, 88, 89, 90, 91, 92 (top), 95, 101, 117, 134, 144 (top and bottom left), 145 (all images), 156, 157 © Shutterstock; page 144 (bottom right) © iStock

Library of Congress Cataloging-in-Publication Data

Names: Dempsey, Rebekah, author.
Title: A blissful nest : designing a stylish and well-loved home / Rebekah Dempsey.
Description: New York : Rock Point, 2021. | Summary: "In *Blissful Nest*, celebrated interior designer Rebekah Dempsey offers hundreds of fresh and attainable design ideas to show you how to discover your interior style and create a home that best reflects your personality and the way you live"—Provided by publisher.
Identifiers: LCCN 2021014152 (print) LCCN 2021014153 (ebook) | ISBN 9781631067273 (hardcover) ISBN 9780760368824 (ebook)
Subjects: LCSH: Interior decoration.
Classification: LCC NK2115 .D485 2021 (print) LCC NK2115 (ebook) | DDC 747—dc23
LC record available at https://lccn.loc.gov/2021014152
LC ebook record available at https://lccn.locgov /2021014153

Printed in China